thegoodwebguide

wine

www.thegoodwebguide.co.uk

thegoodwebguide
wine

Tom Cannavan

The Good Web Guide Limited • London

First Published in Great Britain in 2000 by The Good Web Guide Limited
Broadwall House, 21 Broadwall, London, SE1 9PL

www.thegoodwebguide.co.uk

Email:feedback@thegoodwebguide.co.uk

© 2000 The Good Web Guide Ltd

Text © 2000 Tom Cannavan

Original series concept by Steve Bailey.

Cover photo © Jake Wyman/Photonica

10 9 8 7 6 5 4 3 2 1

A catalogue record for this book is available from the British Library.

ISBN 1-903282-04-7

The publishers and author have done their best to ensure the accuracy and currency of all information in this volume, however they can accept no responsibility for any loss or inconvenience sustained by any reader as a result of its information or advice.

All rights reserved. No part of this publication may be reproduced, transmitted or stored in a retrieval system, in any form or by any means, except for the quotation of brief passages in reviews without permission in writing from The Good Web Guide Ltd.

Project Editor Michelle Clare

Design by Myriad Creative Ltd

Printed in Italy at LEGO S.p.A.

contents

the good web guides	6
introduction	8
user key/key to countries	9
review of the author's site	10
1 wine appreciation	13
2 buying and selling wine	51
3 regions	79
4 wineries	97
5 magazines	115
6 wine accessories	131
glossary of internet terms	146
index	153
how to use your cd	159

the good web guides

The World Wide Web is a vast resource, with millions of sites on every conceivable subject. There are people who have made it their mission to surf the net: cyber-communities have grown, and people have formed relationships and even married on the net.

However, the reality for most people is that they don't have the time or inclination to surf the net for hours on end. Busy people want to use the internet for quick access to information. You don't have to spend hours on the internet looking for answers to your questions and you don't have to be an accomplished net surfer or cyber wizard to get the most out of the web. It can be a quick and useful resource if you are looking for specific information.

The Good Web Guides have been published with this in mind. To give you a head start in your search, our researchers have looked at hundreds of sites and what you will find in the Good Web Guides is a collection of reviews of the best we've found.

The Good Web Guide recommendation is impartial and all the sites have been visited several times. Reviews are focused on the website and what it sets out to do, rather than an endorsement of a company, or their product. A small but beautiful site run by a one-man band may be rated higher than an ambitious but flawed site run by a mighty organisation.

Relevance to the UK-based visitor is also given a high premium: tantalising as it is to read about purchases you can make in California, because of delivery charges, import duties and controls it may not be as useful as a local site.

Our reviewers considered a number of questions when reviewing the sites, such as: How quickly do the sites and individual pages download? Can you move around the site easily and get back to where you started, and do the links work? Is the information up to date and accurate? And is the site pleasing to the eye and easy to read? More importantly, we also asked whether the site has something distinctive to offer, whether it be entertainment, inspiration or pure information. On the basis of the answers to these questions sites are given ratings out of five. As we aim only to include sites that we feel are of serious interest, there are very few low-rated sites.

Bear in mind that the collection of reviews you see here are just a snapshot of the sites at a particular time. The process of choosing and writing about sites is rather like painting the Forth Bridge: as each section appears complete, new sites are launched and others are modified. When you've registered at the Good Web Guide site (see p.159 for further details) you can check out the reviews of new sites and updates of existing ones, or even have them emailed to you. By using the cd rom at the back of the book or registering at our site, you'll find hot links to all the sites listed, so you can just click and go without needing to type the addresses accurately into your browser.

As this is the first edition of the Good Web Guide, all our sites have been reviewed by the author and research team, but we'd like to know what you think. Contact us via the website or email feedback@thegoodwebguide.co.uk. You are welcome to recommend sites, quibble about the ratings, point out changes and inaccuracies or suggest new features to assess.

You can find us at www.thegoodwebguide.co.uk

introduction

How would you describe yourself? Wine lover? Wine enthusiast? Wine collector? Wine investor? Wine taster? Wine buff? Wine bore?

The variety of epithets speaks volumes about why wine and the Web have hit it off so dramatically. Whilst many people drink whisky or beer, very few invest, collect or could happily bore for Britain on the subject. Once bitten by the wine bug there seems to be a fascination that goes far beyond mere lubrication of the throat. We are enthralled by its infinite variety, by the subtle variations caused by grape, place and vintage.

I confess that I have been dismayed by the coverage of wine in many web guides, so the chance to do it properly in a whole book devoted to the subject was irresistible. Most guides offer a lazy listing of the top half dozen sites thrown up by a search on 'wine'. This fails to take account of the reliability, authority and currency of the sites, let alone their ease of use or pertinence to the UK visitor. Clearly such guides are compiled by people who neither know nor love wine.

In researching this guide I visited literally hundreds of sites. Though the task of whittling down the final selection was not easy, my criteria for inclusion were clear and quickly let me sort out the *Moutons* from the wolves. Many sites simply didn't cut the mustard, suffering from poor or insubstantial content, bad design, or being noticeably out of date. A few of the sites I have chosen to include are so simple that they would no doubt be laughed off the screen by the publishers of cutting-edge web sites, pumped full of multimedia steroids. But these small places, often charming and quirky, display an extraordinary knowledge and zeal for their subject.

As a wine lover first and foremost, but also a tremendous enthusiast for the publishing freedom granted to us by the Internet, I have a soft spot for those sites that are non-commercial. Quite a large percentage of the most interesting sites in this guide are the work of passionate individuals. I am sure you will be as astonished as I was by their depth and breadth of coverage. I am also intrigued by the rush towards e-commerce by a plethora of wine merchants, both established and new. I have selected those that are getting things right in terms of the whole shopping experience. Their products and services are of intrinsic interest, but their sites also offer a little more than the hard sell. You will also find numerous resource sites here with something for everyone, from those with a serious academic interest in wine and its development, to those who simply need quick access to good advice and information.

I sincerely hope this guide, and the regularly updated information you will find at www.thegoodwebguide.co.uk, will provide you with many, many hours of surfing pleasure. Remember: as yet there is no law against drinking and surfing, so pour yourself a glass of something interesting, power-up the PC, and let this book guide you to some unique and wonderful wine resources. Cheers.

Tom Cannavan, May 2000

user key

£	Subscription
R	Registration Required
	Secure Online Ordering

key to countries

AUS	Australia
CAN	Canada
FR	France
G	Germany
IRE	Ireland
IS	Israel
IT	Italy
LEB	Lebanon
NZ	New Zealand
SA	South Africa
SIN	Singapore
SP	Spain
SW	Switzerland
SWE	Sweden
UK	United Kingdom
US	United States

tom cannavan's wine pages

Editor's note

When I first thought about who to commission to survey the wine scene on the web, Tom Cannavan was the obvious person to turn to. As a regular visitor to his site, I found out how good and accessible his writing was, and how welcoming he was, even to a newbie oenophile. (When I scored pathetically low on his wine quiz I was both mortified and impressed to discover it was not marked automatically by computer, but by Tom himself.) But all that left me with a dilemma: a guide to the best sites on the web would not be complete without a full review of The Wine Pages, though I could not reasonably expect the modest, self-effacing Mr Cannavan to blow his own trumpet. So we're doing it for him. Under any other circumstances it would rate as a five star site and a must-see destination for wine-lovers on the web. So here, undeniably partisan, but with ample justification, is the Good Web Guide style review of Tom's site.

Tom Cannavan's Wine Pages
www.wine-pages.com

Category: Enthusiasts

UK

Tom Cannavan has published his Wine Pages site since 1996, since when it has become globally recognised as one of the very best. Updated daily; the site has over 3000 pages of information; two thousand tasting notes; a friendly and thriving UK discussion group; a complete illustrated wine course and free monthly prize competitions. But it is the sheer breadth of the coverage and the author's expertise that sets this site apart from the pack. As well as his obvious knowledge, Tom brings to the site tremendous enthusiasm and a wonderfully down-to-earth style.

SPECIAL FEATURES

Tasting notes provides possibly the largest collection of tasting notes from a single palate on the Web. Everything is here, from rare and outlandishly expensive old clarets, to a host of affordable wines obtainable on the UK high street. Tasting notes are divided into Notes from Organised Tastings, Notes from Restaurants and Notes from My Cellar, the latter further sub-divided into world regions. Most of these come complete with a label image and advice on when to drink. Each review is dated. And the standard is extremely high and consistent.

Wine of the Week is published each weekend and features a moderately-priced wine that has particularly impressed. Every Wine of the Week has a label image, as well as UK prices and stockists. These weekly bottles have built into a wonderful back-catalogue of everyday wine recommendations which can be printed off as a very useful shopping list. You'll find the past Wines of the Week archived under the heading Cheapies.

Course is the introduction to wine appreciation that Tom teaches both privately and at the University of Glasgow. Here, you can access all the course notes for free. These clear introductions, complete with illustrations, form one of the most comprehensive educational resources on the Web. Just one of the many interactive features to be found on the site is a collection of Quizzes. These can be used to test your knowledge having completed the course, or just for the fun of it.

Regions Introductory articles on all the world's most important wine regions. Each is minutely detailed, and comes complete with a map, photographs and illustrations. A list of recommended wines and producers is also included.

Food and Wine is an extensive collection of articles culled from one of Tom's terrestrial magazine columns. Each takes a food topic in turn, Wine with Cheese for example, and discusses general wine matching options, as well as recommending half a dozen specific wines. UK prices and stockists are quoted.

Wine News pertains specifically to UK visitors. It lists public tasting events, wine sales and other items of interest across Britain. Typical items are a diary of tasting events and Tom's tips for the best bargains in current supermarket promotions.

The UK Forum is the meeting place for a friendly, but very knowledgeable set of wine lovers looking to discuss their favourite subject from a UK viewpoint. The standard of debate here is high, and conducted in a civil manner.

Books contains a selection of several dozen wine books, each reviewed in depth and rated. All books have a photograph of the jacket, as well as price, ISBN number and a direct link to an on-line seller of the book, if available.

Dining encompasses Cannavan's other passion. Here are full reviews of scores of UK restaurants he sees fit to recommend. The descriptions are as entertaining as they are useful. This is another section that could be printed off and used very easily as a reference guide. There are also a couple of dozen restaurants visited on Tom's world wide travels.

Visitors' Tips Worldwide visitors send in their own recommendations for reasonably priced wines they have enjoyed. Though most reviews are British, they come from places as far afield as Australia, Canada and even Puerto Rico! Each has a tasting note, local stockists and prices. Visitors' Tips seem to be added very regularly.

Travel is a small collection of guides to touring the world's wine regions. Though these are few in number, they are packed with useful information and addresses, as well as being entertaining reads in their own right.

Tasting Notes is an archive of several hundred notes supplied by Forum members, and harvested from on-line discussions.

Who's Who offers autobiographical profiles of your fellow surfers, and you may add your own if you intend to contribute.

OTHER FEATURES

Vintage Chart Courtesy of American wine writer Robert Parker. Wines are awarded marks out of 100 for quality, for vintages dating back to 1970.

Wine Online Links to a selection of the author's favourite sites, including personal sites, UK wine merchants and a couple of his favourite sites that have nothing to do with wine at all.

About Me Short biography of the author.

Press Extensive mantelpiece collection of glowing press reviews and web awards.

Even if Tom weren't the author of this book, his site would easily deserve a five-star rating. It has proved itself over the past five years, in which time it has grown into an enormously impressive web destination for the wine lover, particularly with its clean and simple design, reliable information and, of course, its policy of daily updates. Very highly recommended.

Chapter 1

wine appreciation

What is it about wine lovers and the Web? There is no other food or beverage subject that inspires so many to put virtual pen to cyber paper in order to describe, discuss and eulogise so passionately about their obsessions.

True, there are many sites on other alcoholic drinks, but only a fraction of the thousands devoted to wine. Perhaps it's because wine itself is such a multifaceted subject. It appeals on so many levels, from the casual drinker seeking the best bargain on the supermarket shelf, to the dedicated collector in search of the fine and rare.

Without a doubt this band of enthusiasts provides one of the very best resources for the online wine lover. Many of these are amateur 'hobby' sites that are quite staggering in their level of expertise and professionalism. An extraordinary wealth of material is offered-up freely, simply in order that others might share the author's passion.

There are sites which are virtual magazines with weekly or even daily updates, others that are huge repositories of reference materials, and yet others that host thriving interactive communities. Some combine all three to offer a truly significant resource for the wine lover.

Whatever your level of interest or your own particular area of wine obsession, the browsing fields of the enthusiasts — the amateurs du vin — provide some very rich pickings indeed.

www.vine2wine.com			
Vine2Wine			
Overall rating: ★★★★★			
Classification:	Links	Readability:	★★★★
Updating:	Frequently	Content:	★★★★★
Navigation:	★★★★★	Speed:	★★★★
CAN			

Vine2wine is nothing more than a huge database of links to wine sites worldwide. However, not only is it extremely comprehensive, but every site is reviewed and rated and, best of all, kept bang up to date. Site reviews are brief, pithy and to the point, succinctly summing up the pros and cons of a site. Researching the enormous number of sites covered by vine2wine must be a Herculean task. Keeping up to date with changes must be just as daunting, but by and large this is done extremely competently: broken links are few and far between, and if a site is recommended it is usually well worth some of your surfing time.

The site uses a navigation panel on the left-hand edge of the screen that provides links to all sections. Some of these sections are sub-divided into dozens of listings. A temporary menu of these replaces the navigation panel, but Main Link Menu at the top of the screen will take you straight back.

SPECIAL FEATURES

Wine Links is what vine2wine is all about. This is a moderated directory of resources, not a search engine. Although it doesn't include all the world's wine sites, it is a huge collection. Basically, if it's not listed here, it's probably not worth listing. The links are divided into a dozen categories, including Groups and Clubs, Personal Pages and Publications. There are also excellent links to wineries, wine shops and a whole host of wine-related information, commerce and appreciation sites. Each site is rated between one and three stars, representing the amount of information contained. A brief pen-picture highlights each site's major features.

Featured sites are chosen every month or two. A site is selected as one of the very best on the Web and highlighted in a little more depth. This has built into a fine collection of those sites that are reference points for the online wine-lover.

OTHER FEATURES

There's a **News** page, useful if you only visit occasionally as it gives details of any changes or major additions to the site. There is a **Site Search** facility too, but this adds little as the alphabetic listings within the site's categories are an efficient way to access information.

Vine2wine has been around for a while under various guises and a recent makeover has not only improved its functionality, but has given it a very smart look and feel. At the end of the day, however, it is the quality and reliability of information that sets the site apart from similar listings sites.

www.bath.ac.uk/~su3ws/wine-faq/
The Wine FAQ

Overall rating: ★★★★			
Classification: Enthusiasts		**Readability:**	★★★★
Updating:	Occasionally	**Content:**	★★★★
Navigation:	★★★★	**Speed:**	★★★★

(US)

The Wine FAQ (Frequently Asked Questions) is a no-nonsense resource that aims to provide succinct explanations and factual information on a whole host of wine-related subjects. Whilst it did indeed start life as a series of questions and answers, it has evolved into a pretty comprehensive encyclopedia of wine data and has lost its strict question/answer format. This allows more flexibility. The writing style is factual and quite casual, but there is good information and it's very easy to spend half an hour browsing through the material.

The author, Bradford Brown, is modest about his knowledge and puts a *caveat emptor* sign right up front, reminding readers that he is an enthusiast, not a learned professor or wine professional. Having said that, we found the information to be accurate and unbiased.

The opening screen has links to the brief overviews of the site and its creators (under the Welcome and Design tags), but the guts of the Wine FAQ are accessed by clicking Table of Contents or Index. These two options allow you to use the site in two distinct and flexible ways. The former can be employed simply to browse through the material, reading topics in a logical and progressive fashion. This makes for a comprehensive educational experience that would be an ideal primer for the beginner. The latter, encyclopedia-like approach is extremely useful as a quick reference guide: if you come across a wine-related term that's unfamiliar, use this A-Z as a quick look-up facility.

Load speeds are quite good. The site is just a few large text files which are accessed at appropriate places from the index. The original site is in California; the website address given above is a mirror site at the University of Bath. Much of the reference data is fairly static, but entries are updated and expanded occasionally.

SPECIAL FEATURES

The Wine FAQ This section is nothing more than a computerised version of an exhaustive encyclopedia of wine reference material. This material ranges from succinct lists and tables of data (like a rundown on grape varieties) to more opinionated pieces on controversial subjects like cork-taint in wines. There are also more extensive, discursive pieces on topics such as 'What is Wine?' or 'Aging Wine' that act as useful and comprehensive guides for the wine novice.

The wine FAQ is widely regarded as one of the best wine reference works on the Web. This is not a flashy site. It is very straightforward in its presentation, a little old-fashioned in its look and feel and it makes no attempt to get out there and grab your attention. What you have is an extremely useful and well-informed reference work that you can take down off the shelf, dust off and use whenever you need to. A very valuable resource.

www.wine-lovers-page.com
The Wine Lovers' Page

Overall rating: ★★★★			
Classification:	Enthusiasts	Readability:	★★★★
Updating:	Daily	Content:	★★★★★
Navigation:	★★★	Speed:	★★★★

US

This site is run by Robin Garr, a well-known journalist and wine writer who has been involved in online wine appreciation since the mid-eighties, when he was manager of Compuserve's wine forum. The Wine Lovers' Page is part-co-operative, with wine-tasting notes, articles and special features supplied by a global circle of amateur wine nuts. Generally, the standard is extremely high. The rest of the material is Garr's own, and his guides, reviews and recommendations are utterly reliable. The site is updated on an almost daily basis, with both the author's writings and key excerpts from recent threads on the site's Discussion Group.

The site is packed with features and articles that are well laid-out and load quickly due to sensible use of graphics. Often, longer pieces are sub-divided and a menu opens up in a separate frame allowing you to visit each sub-section in turn.

As one of the most comprehensive wine resources on the Web the sheer volume of data can make this sprawling site seem rather unwieldy. The over-long home page offers many options: scrolling down through the first couple of screens reveals a lengthy selection of headline links to the site's latest additions. Only then will you come to a banner proclaiming 'Welcome to the Wine Lovers' Page' and 'Where would you like to begin?' This introduces the navigation centre proper, with links to each of the site's main sub-sections. Generally, all lower-level pages have buttons for

Home. Indeed, returning Home en route to visiting a new section is my tip to avoid confusion, but this site requires a bit of a rethink on its overall navigation strategy. Downloading pages is speedy enough, considering the volume of the content on some of them.

One useful feature of the site is an audio pronunciation guide for tricky wine and grape names. This requires an MP3 player for access, though thoughtfully, links to download sites are provided.

SPECIAL FEATURES

Each of these is accessible from the main navigation centre towards the bottom of the home page.

Wine Lover's Discussion Group A sophisticated bulletin board service where wine-lovers from around the globe can meet to discuss wine-related issues. This is not a chat room with live conversation, but a public forum where participants can see and respond to a whole series of discussions and debates on wine. The large body of knowledgeable participants includes amateur enthusiasts, wine-makers, writers and wine merchants. The discussion group is a phenomenal success, with debate of high quality. The civilised, welcoming and good-humoured tone is set by Garr who deftly moderates discussions. This is a delightful place to hang out for the wired-up wine lover, even though a lot of the discussion is rather US-centred.

Wine Tasting Notes Archive This archive now boasts over 50,000 tasting notes, mostly garnered from the discussion group above, on everything from cheap and cheerful bottles, to the world's greatest and rarest fine wines. Possibly the largest repository of tasting notes on the web, with a useful search facility.

Wine Tasting Toolbox Everything you need to know about wine tasting, from a rundown on techniques and scoring systems, to tips on how to organise fun wine-tasting events. Everything is written in plain English and the advice is sound.

The 30 Second Wine Advisor For drinkers in a hurry perhaps? Sign up here and the author will send you a free weekly email with a brief and tasty selection of wine notes, wine tips and a link to the wine site of the week. This is a clever idea that is well executed.

Links A long list of international links, sub-divided into commercial and non-commercial categories, and each presented along with Robin Garr's brief comments. He also bestows his own personal 'Top 10 per cent of all wine websites' award to outstanding non-commercial efforts.

OTHER FEATURES

There is a wealth of information and reference material on this site. This includes a collection of wine articles and essays by various contributors; the **Wine Questionary** where common questions about wine are answered; the **Wine Label Decoder** where the mysteries of the wine label are unravelled; and a **Wine Lovers Chat Room** that assembles twice a week for live wine-based conversation.

Despite the occasional inconsistency in look and feel and the rather haphazard organisation, this remains an exemplary site in terms of content, expertise and objective advice. The author's gentle yet authoritative presence is felt throughout the interactive areas, and everyone from beginner to expert will find something to delight. Very highly recommended: a benchmark site.

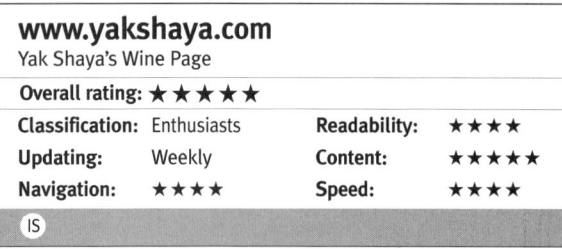

www.yakshaya.com
Yak Shaya's Wine Page

Overall rating: ★★★★		
Classification: Enthusiasts	Readability:	★★★★
Updating: Weekly	Content:	★★★★★
Navigation: ★★★★	Speed:	★★★★

Rather immodestly, amateur wine-nut Yak Shaya describes himself as 'a Burgundy-wine buff par-excellence'. His page is a celebration of all things Yak, but his infectious enthusiasm — as well as his formidable palate — endear him to the reader prepared to spend a few minutes getting to know the man and his site. English is not his first language and he begs your forgiveness for the mistakes in his writing, but these are no worse than many sites written by Americans or Brits on the web. There is certainly plenty to browse on the site: writings about wine, food and Shaya's adventures, which makes it a highly enjoyable read.

Shaya presents a comprehensive guide to the Burgundy region and its wines that is as authoritative as any text book. His wine tasting notes are of course entirely subjective, but there is no doubt that he is an immensely experienced taster whose judgement and consistency appear reliable.

The site layout has a consistent approach and simply constructed pages. A navigation bar at the top of every page links to all sub-sections. On long pages the bar is repeated at the bottom.

SPECIAL FEATURES

Tasting Note Archive is the collected and ever-expanding repository of Shaya's tasting notes. Predominantly, these are for Burgundy wines, though he has, in his own words,

been attempting a foray into other wine regions. Notes are presented by region, and within each region in strict alphabetical order. Don't come here looking for a supermarket bottle to go with the weekend pizza: Shaya has hedonistic tastes and there's only a handful of notes on 'cheap' (£20) village Burgundies, but super-expensive Grand Cru wines fill screen after screen. Every wine is rated with marks out of 20 (see 'Yak's rating scale' for a precise definition). There is also a nice and far less exacting concluding rating: 'Buy More?' which rates every wine as a 'Yes', 'No' or 'Maybe.' These notes offer glimpses into a wine-drinking world to which most of us could only aspire.

Burgundy 'Primer' Shaya's home turf is Burgundy, and this

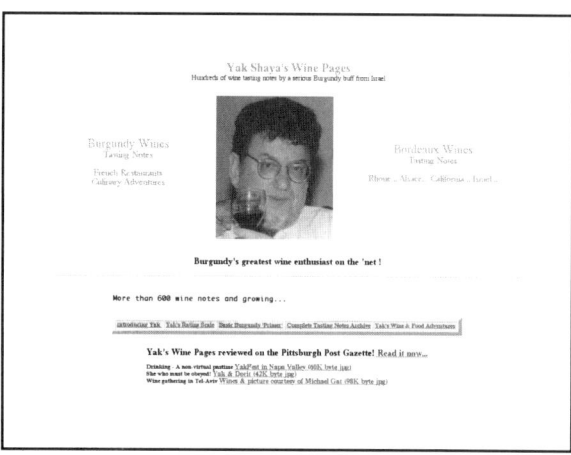

extensive introduction to the complexities of the region is well done, if a touch dry. It attempts to unravel the intricacies of Burgundy's labelling and system of classification: a tough task in this most confusing of all French wine regions. There are good descriptions of all the major communes and recommendations for producers within each. Typical of

Shaya's high-flying style is that 'lesser' Burgundy regions of the Mâconnais and Côte Chalonnaise are completely ignored, as indeed is Chablis.

Wine & Food Adventures Come with Shaya as he takes you on fabulous gastronomic adventures. You can experience the vicarious pleasures of dinner for four at Paris's three-star Taillevent, but thankfully not the pleasure of the bill ($1050). Or re-live Shaya's 50th birthday celebrations: a modest eight-course affair, starting with Dom Perignon, finishing with 1948 Taylors Port and finding time for Yquem, Cheval Blanc and Montrachet amongst others in between.

OTHER FEATURES

A section entitled **Introducing Yak**, and an explanation of his wine scoring system.

There is an absolute mountain of wine-related material on this site. Rarely is each of the 600 plus fine wine tasting notes presented simply as a factual description of the stuff in the bottle: more often there is a description of the events surrounding its drinking, or a little mini-essay on the wine and its background. This site is very much a 'YakFest' and as much about the man as the wine, but it is highly readable and extremely entertaining.

www.bipin.com
Bipin's Wine Notes

Overall rating: ★★★★			
Classification:	Enthusiasts	**Readability:**	★★★★
Updating:	Quarterly	**Content:**	★★★
Navigation:	★★★	**Speed:**	★★★★

(US)

Bipin Desai is a Professor at the University of California and amongst the world's great amateurs du vin. His site, launched in Spring 2000, is a response to countless requests he has had to write down his decades of experience tasting the world's greatest wines. As he says, 'Having organised as many comprehensive tastings as I have over the past 18 years, and tasted as many great wines as I have, it is perhaps worth writing something about them.' This site is essentially very simple, being nothing much more than a collection of notes on wines, food and people he has known. Most of us could only dream of moving in the tasting circles that Desai frequents, so here is the chance to share, at least vicariously, in a few of them.

SPECIAL FEATURES

1900 Château Margaux A Personal Odyssey This great wine was the one that started it all for Desai and has haunted his wine drinking ever since (in the nicest possible way). He has acquired and drunk the wine with a passion ever since, and through that process has shared it with some of the world's greatest wine figures, from Corinne Mentzelopoulos (the owner of Margaux) to Francis Ford Coppola. This essay describes the circumstances that have surrounded his most memorable bottles.

Skeletons in my Closet is the story of how Desai stumbled across something that felt like wood underneath a pile of linen in one of his closets: 'When I pulled it out I was ecstatic at what I saw. It was a wooden case, without the lid, of 24 half bottles, mostly Lafite, Mouton Rothschild, Pichon Lalande and other Châteaux from 1961 and 1962.' If the chances of you making such a happy discovery — forgotten for 20 years — are slim, why not read how this turned out once the bottles were opened?

OTHER FEATURES

Each of the small collection of essays makes for fascinating reading. Mostly these are tales of the finest wines and the grand occasions, but Desai's obvious love and enthusiasm for wine carry these comfortably beyond the rather shallow Lifestyles of the Rich and Famous territory. His comparison of the 1985 and 1986 vintages in Bordeaux, for example, is as considered an account as you will find anywhere.

There's nothing flashy about this site. It is essentially a collection of essays gathered under a simple index page. It is the straightforward but passionate account of how one privileged wine lover has tasted his way through some extraordinary wines. It will appeal most to those with an interest in the world's great wines, particularly clarets.

www.marksquires.com
Mark Squires' E-zine on Wine

Overall rating: ★ ★ ★ ★			
Classification:	Enthusiasts	Readability:	★ ★ ★ ★
Updating:	Weekly	Content:	★ ★ ★ ★
Navigation:	★ ★ ★	Speed:	★ ★ ★ ★

(US)

This was one of the web's earliest wine appreciation sites. Mark Squires is a Philadelphia lawyer who has been running the site since 1995 (positively mediaeval in web terms). Its organisation is a little haphazard and visually it is rather garish, but there is a body of excellent material here that outweighs those nit-picks.

Squires has scores of spiky, subjective and thought-provoking articles on the world of wine within the site. These are well-written and entertaining. Squires knows his wine very well and has travelled widely in the USA and Europe to gain first-hand impressions of wines, wine regions and wine-makers. Naturally, some of the older tasting notes and articles from the mid 1990s can't be relied upon for prices.

On each page you will find colourful link buttons to the site's half dozen main areas: Home, Introduction, Wine, Interactive, Fun Stuff and Search. Sometimes these are located at the top of the page, sometimes in a panel on the left-hand side. Within each main section there is a further index. On entering the site a Recent Updates page spotlights the newest information, so regular visitors will probably go there first.

Download speed is good, with larger articles or photo collections broken down into manageable chunks.

SPECIAL FEATURES

Bulletin Boards This is the site's discussion area, which is lively and entertaining. There is a nice sense of community here, though that community is strongly rooted in the USA and the discussion is naturally biased towards Amercian news and viewpoints. The opinions and advice on offer are reliable.

Wine Articles As befits a Philadelphia lawyer perhaps, Squires makes some powerful arguments on a whole host of contentious issues within this, his own favourite section of the site. It is a collection of longer pieces on topics such as wine pricing, prohibition and the collecting of fashionable wines as trophies.

Tasting Notes These are grouped by year from 1995 onward. Within each year notes are listed by month and then by country of origin. This is as good a way as any to deal with such a huge collection of notes and there is also a search facility. Squires writes his notes well and awards each wine a score out of 100.

Wine Quotes An entertaining collection of quotes from famous and not-so-famous historical and literary figures. There's always something here to amuse.

The Photo Archive Squires is a passionate photographer and there's a large collection here, not only of wine-related photos, but of more general subjects too. Some earlier photos have been deliberately reduced in quality in a trade-off for faster loading which, with today's faster modems, is a bit of a pity.

OTHER FEATURES

Wine Basics for Beginners is a solid and reliable run through issues such as storage, decanting and preserving leftover wine.

Best Buys lists inexpensive wines that have earned the best scores from Squires, but UK stockists aren't given. The site has a collection of wine-related Audio Clips from TV and radio that are amusing, but need a basic sound player like Windows Media Player.

A content-rich site that proves very rewarding, once you take time to explore it. Very wordy at times, it will certainly appeal to the wine-nut rather than the casual imbiber. The US focus restricts the usefulness of some information, but there's just so much of it that it well-deserves its inclusion here.

www2.wildfire.com/~ag/portwine/			
Port Wine			
Overall rating: ★★★★			
Classification:	Enthusiasts	**Readability:**	★★★★
Updating:	Varies	**Content:**	★★★★★
Navigation:	★★★★	**Speed:**	★★★

(US)

This is a fantastically well-researched celebration of the great port wines of Portugal, and Keith Gabryelski's passion for his subject is writ large on every page of his site. There are comparative tables, a mass of statistics, reams of facts and explanations of obscure port terms and technology. The History section maps out major landmarks in the development of port back to 1095, for example, and the section on How Port is Made is beautifully illustrated and exhaustively detailed. Gabryelski's writing style is factual, efficient and authorative. There are no literary fireworks, but his style is very approachable and easy to follow. It's also backed up by frequent references and links to other official websites.

The site uses a clever navigation frame on the left-hand side of the screen. It has links to the various main sections of the site. Some of the links are marked with a symbol indicating that they can be expanded to show lower levels: click the symbol and a hierarchical list of further links will open up. This can be closed again with a second click on the symbol.

Each main section of the site has been created as one long page. In fact, when the expand/collapse facility is used on a section in the navigation panel, all of the expanded sub-options that appear are simply links to different points within the same long page. This has been done to make it possible to print out a whole section without having to piece together separate pages, but it does mean that loading larger sections (Producers for example) takes an age; literally minutes at average modem speeds.

Gabryelski states that the site is constantly growing as he adds new vintage data. Having said that, most of the information is fairly static reference material.

SPECIAL FEATURES

Customs This succinct beginner's guide to port is a chance to mug-up on topics like how to store port, how to decant and serve port, appropriate stemware for drinking port and what should be served to accompany port, from cheeses to cigars (apparently it is *de rigueur* to light up only during the second glass).

How Port is Made is a terrific explanation of the intricacies of the process, from grape growing to bottling. It is illustrated with helpful photographs, diagrams and tables. There's a rundown on the grapes of port, the climate and geography of the Douro Valley (where port grapes are grown) and a very thorough piece on the regulations that govern the production of the different styles of port.

Producers Within this enormous and exhaustive listing Gabryelski includes details of literally hundreds of port producers. For each he includes contact details and website if they have one, visiting information, a roll-call of the vintages they have declared over the past century or more and a logo or label image. He also awards his own subjective star rating from one (below average quality) to four (superior quality) for each.

History A well-presented section that takes a timeline for port going back to the eleventh century and pauses at all the major milestone years explaining particular events that have shaped the beverage we know today.

Styles Concise explanation of the sometimes bewildering range of port styles that might be encountered. The differences are explained, in terms of quality, production methods and ageability.

OTHER FEATURES

Vineyards All port vineyards are graded using seven criteria including geographic position, climatic conditions, altitude, type of soil and age of vines. Vineyards lists all of them with their grades.

Some of the other features listed in the navigation index look interesting, but unfortunately need to be fleshed-out. The section on **Port Style Wines,** for example, looks at equivalent wines from around the world, but at the moment is a brief paragraph with a promise that more will be added over time.

There really is a lot of material in this site. The detailed and technical sections on history, producers and vineyards, will appeal mostly to port buffs, but the more general introductions to how port is made and its customs and styles are very comprehensive and have been done very nicely.

www.wineanorak.com
The Wine Anorak

Overall rating: ★★★★			
Classification:	Enthusiasts	Readability:	★★★★
Updating:	Weekly	Content:	★★★★★
Navigation:	★★★★	Speed:	★★★★

UK

The quality of the writing in this site is generally very good indeed, distinguishing it from many. The author, Jamie Goode, a London-based wine lover, clearly knows and loves his subject. As well as useful facts and figures, there's a lot of personal opinion on this site, but points of view are always well argued and entertaining. There is plenty to read, from tasting notes to long polemics on controversial issues, though Goode does get a bit wordy at times and the longer pieces sometimes get a little bogged down. There is liberal use of high-quality photos, but not too many to make speed of loading a problem.

The attractive homepage features a sidebar with navigation buttons to each of the site's dozen sections. Another set of links to these same sections is positioned centre screen, each with a brief synopsis of what you'll find there. On the right is Don't Miss, a selection of the author's chosen highlights. Unfortunately, there is a little inconsistency as the sidebar disappears within some sections. It would also be nice if there were navigation options at the bottom of long pages to save scrolling back to the top.

SPECIAL FEATURES

Wine UK This is treated like a separate site, with a different colour scheme and its own navigation bar. Information here is of specific interest to UK-based wine lovers, with a useful and extensive list of wine merchants complete with contact details, a set of recommended wines which is updated monthly, and the collected tasting notes of the author, most of which are for wines available on the high street.

Features Features and essays on wine regions, wine-making and issues such as terroir, wine competitions and the status

of English wine-making. This is building into a solid body of serious and contemplative writings on wine-related issues, many of which are illustrated.

Wine Photos The author's other passion is utilised with a collection of wine and vineyard photography. The slide show from the world's vine-growing regions is excellent, though the resolution could be higher and the images smaller.

Wine Travel Tales of the author's wine travels through France, California and Australia. These are entertaining and informative, with lots of photos to accompany the text and several addresses which should be very useful if you're planning a wine-related holiday. There's also general advice on wine-touring holidays which pinpoints the regions to visit and warns you of the formalities of visiting the winemakers.

Food and Wine A bit of a mish-mash, with everything from fondue recipes to the author's attempts to find something to go with salmon in Hollandaise sauce. Having said that, the short collection of articles offers some good specific suggestions as well as general guidelines.

OTHER FEATURES

Tasting Notes on inexpensive and moderately priced wines from around the world are reliable and are presented categorised by region.

The Book Reviews section casts a critical and incisive eye over a dozen or so titles with no holds barred in the author's trustworthy opinions.

Links presents a small but carefully chosen list of wine sites along with the author's brief summary and comments on each.

Controversies is an intriguing-sounding section, but for now merely repeats a selection of the articles also to be found under the **Features** heading.

This site has been around for a while, but a fresh new look for 2000 has made it much more attractive and easier to use. It perhaps lacks a bit of substance, spreading content a little thin, but the mix of factual reference material and intelligent, thought-provoking articles gives the site more breadth and depth than most. Another not to miss.

www.veronafiere.it/slowines
Slow Food Guide to Wine

Overall rating: ★ ★ ★ ★			
Classification:	Magazine	Readability:	★ ★ ★ ★ ★
Updating:	Infrequently	Content:	★ ★ ★ ★ ★
Navigation:	★ ★ ★ ★	Speed:	★ ★ ★

(IT)

Slow Food is an Italian movement, established in 1989 by Carlo Petrini. Petrini founded Slow Food when McDonalds opened a branch in Rome and the organisation is dedicated to preserving a philosophy of enjoyment and appreciation of the finer things in life, specifically good food and wine. Slow Food celebrates regionality and authenticity, and now boasts 40,000 members worldwide who receive its magazine four times per year.

There is some excellent information here: the maps and guides are a tremendous resource. The extensive introductions to the world's wine regions and the profiles of wineries are thorough and professional. The style is fairly straight-laced and textbookish, but not at all dry, and they are written in plain English.

The site is well thought-out, with links to the site's half-dozen sub-sections on the homepage. Go first to Help. Here you will see a little diagram that explains how to navigate the site, and a How To Use This Guide page which explains the symbols employed to indicate type, quality and price of wines reviewed. All pages feature the same navigation links.

The magazine-like format relies on images on practically every page. Though these result in a little delay, it is quite acceptable at average modem speeds and the pictures do greatly enhance the articles.

SPECIAL FEATURES

Catalogue The oddly named Catalogue is not a sales brochure, but the main content area of the site. Here you will find entries for each of the world's significant wine-producing countries. Clicking any one reveals an annotated map of the country showing the wine-producing areas, and summary information such as vineyard area, export figures and principal grape varieties.

Wineries is a very comprehensive list of producers for that country/region. Clicking one of these brings up a detailed introduction to the producer, including contact details. Below the introduction are honest and accurate tasting notes, usually for several vintages of that producer's wines. The Slow Wine symbols are employed to indicate style, quality and price range.

Description offers excellent introductions to the country or region and its wines. These detailed notes encompass history, geography and lots of in-depth information on grapes, styles and regional characteristics.

Top Wines reveals a similar opening screen to Catalogue, with entries for major wine-producing countries. Here are gathered all of the wines awarded 'three bunches' - the top award in Slow Wine's wine-quality rating system. France for example lists 60 wines or so. For each, a label image is displayed — which is a nice touch — as well as a tasting note and winery contact details.

The Slow Food guide is a terrific resource that links together the best wine regions, producers and wine reviews. It is nicely and intelligently written and works well. The only drawbacks are reservations over its frequency of updating and the fact that the content, though dealing comprehensively with what it covers, is limited.

www.stratsplace.com
Strat's Place

Overall rating: ★★★★			
Classification: Enthusiasts		**Readability:**	★★★
Updating: Weekly		**Content:**	★★★★
Navigation: ★★★		**Speed:**	★★★

(US)

This multifaceted site by Art and Betsy Stratermeyer expresses the authors', love of wine, gardening and the arts. The Wine section is the most extensive, built principally from thousands of contributions from wine lovers around the world. It is without doubt one of the largest wine sites on the web, but because it is really a large repository of contributions from a multitude of different sources, the standard does vary. Overall, however, it is extremely good. The sheer volume of data here means there are often second or third opinions available on any given topic.

The homepage introduces each of the site's Main Topics (The World of Wine, Gardening and The Arts). Once inside The World of Wine you will find a What's New section for regular readers, and below that a grid which has links to the main sub-sections. At the bottom of every page a navigation panel provides links to home and each of the site's Main Topic sections.

Index pages load quickly, but the large size of some lower-level pages can make downloads a bit ponderous. The same goes for searches on the site's larger databases.

The audio Pronunciation Guide section requires sound capability for simple '.wav' files. This should come as standard with your computer.

SPECIAL FEATURES

The Wine Cellar Picture Album Several dozen visitors have sent photos and details of how they store their wines, from elaborate, high-tech and money-no-object mini-palaces, to basic under-stair solutions. If you have a particular problem in storing wines, you're almost certain to find some neat solutions here.

Wine Label Library Presented by country of origin, this is a collection of over 1,000 wine labels. The quality of the images is highly variable, but it is a fairly comprehensive collection.

The Wine 'How To' Section Useful topics like 'How to hold a wine tasting', 'Removing labels from bottles', 'Removing wine stains' and 'Selecting and cleaning glassware.'

Rogov's Ramblings The Stratermeyers give part of their site over to the ruminations of Daniel Rogov, an Israeli wine lover and *bon viveur*. This section of the site alone is worthy of an entry in its own right, with a huge collection of writings. An example would be the rather dull sounding 'A Few Words About Wine Bottles' which turns out to be a fascinating and thoroughly researched piece on how cultural, historical and economic forces shaped the wine bottle as we know it.

You Know You're a Wine Nut if ... A collection of witty, and occasionally too close to home, definitions: 'You sniff the cork notice board at work', 'You give the communion wine a numerical rating', 'You find yourself swirling a glass of water.'

OTHER FEATURES

The Glossary of Wine Tasting Terms and **Glossary of Grape Varieties** are extensive and useful resources.

Wine and Food Pairings lists scores of foods/recipes and gives wine-matching suggestions from numerous contributors.

The Living Wine Dictionary explains many wine-related terms, with an audio pronunciation guide to many.

There is a folksy and very welcoming feel to this lovely site. Art and Betsy's visitors are treated as an extended family and the authors' love of wine and obvious joy in sharing it with an online community set this site apart from many. You may find it a little unwieldy to use, and the standard is a little variable, but it is charming and down to earth as well as being packed with information.

www.bboxbbs.ch/home/tbm
TBM's Wine Links

Overall rating: ★★★★			
Classification: Links		**Readability:**	★★★
Updating:	Regularly	**Content:**	★★★
Navigation:	★★★★★	**Speed:**	★★★★

(SW)

TBM is an otherwise anonymous Swiss enthusiast who provides another directory of wine links on the web. To qualify, sites must be non-commercial (no merchants or traders).This is another truly excellent resource which takes a different approach to Vine2wine, and has a couple of nice features which really distinguish it. It is very reliable and updated meticulously.

SPECIAL FEATURES

General Wine Links is the first category of links listed. It is divided into sub-categories like General Wine Info, Wine Tasting and Wine Labels. Within each are dozens, possibly scores of entries. One of the nicest features of TBM's site is that he indicates the language of the site with a small symbol (a blue 'E' for English) and he highlights particularly interesting or comprehensive sites with a red star.

Continents and Countries is an extremely useful and unique collection of links. Entries are listed alphabetically (from Argentina to Zimbabwe) and for each, TBM lists general information sites, winery sites and regional search engines that might help you home in on specific data. Once again, the star sites and the language symbols are employed. This is particularly useful within this section, where of the eleven German information sites listed, for example, you can pick out a glance the five with English-language content.

Newsgroups features a collection of links to a dozen or so discussion groups on the Internet. Some are general wine appreciation groups, others specific to a wine or a country. Clicking on a link will open up your browser's Newsgroup tool and take you straight to the list of current messages.

TBM provides an invaluable service with his comprehensive and very easy-to-use site. The strategy he employs for cataloguing his links complements the Vine2wine resource, and between them there simply isn't much for the wine lover on the web that isn't included.

www.wineontheweb
Wine on the Web

Overall rating: ★★★★			
Classification:	Enthusiasts	**Readability:**	★★★★
Updating:	Infrequently	**Content:**	★★★★
Navigation:	★★★★	**Speed:**	★★★

UK

This British site by wine writer Andrew Jones has a good deal of high-quality, if not especially distinctive, content. However there are a couple of unique features that really distinguish it, including a talking-book section of wine reports that would be a boon for visually-impaired wine lovers. The site is clear and uncluttered, navigation is simple using the panel to the left of screen, and though a little gimmicky for my taste with half a dozen animations on some screens, loading speeds are acceptable.

SPECIAL FEATURES

Radio Postcard is a collection of audio reports on subjects like Vinopolis, the London wine theme-park, or on Champagne, recorded in the cellars of Charles Heidsieck. Jones files such reports for broadcast on a network of local radio stations and the quality of both audio presentation and content is excellent. Usually, there are interviews with winemakers or figures from the wine trade and Jones has an infectious enthusiasm for his subjects. These are entertaining for all, but undeniably useful for the visually impaired; you should play these files using the Windows Media Player or similar. A download button is provided for those who need a player, and the process is quite painless.

Psion Users is the site's second unique feature. Here, those with the popular Psion personal organiser can download the database of tasting notes from the site to carry with them as they shop. The site has only a couple of hundred tasting notes, and many of these are for vintages no longer available in the shops, but it is still a clever and worthwhile utility.

A-Z is an alphabetical list of tasting notes, almost all for everyday wines. There's a label image, tasting note and score out of 100, plus usually a nice little bit of background on the wine or winery.

Features is a small collection of writings on subjects as diverse as 'Norwegian Pinot Noir at latitude 60° North' to 'Dom Perignon, the Champagne and the man.' These are full-length, fact-filled pieces that are interesting and entertaining.

OTHER FEATURES

Includes a **Wine News** page, with snippets of useful or amusing information, **Vintage Charts** for the world's major regions, and a small collection of rather disparate articles gathered under the heading **Consumer Advice**. There's a section of the site devoted to **Beer and Whisky**, and an opportunity to buy some wine **Books**.

A stylish and well constructed site. The audio reports and whizzy Psion download add great appeal and are unique selling points. The rest of the site needs to be beefed out a little, but that is not to deny its usefulness, nor the quality in evidence.

www.wine-people.com
Wine People

Overall rating: ★★★★			
Classification:	Enthusiasts	Readability:	★★★★
Updating:	Weekly	Content:	★★★★
Navigation:	★★★★	Speed:	★★★★

(US)

Arthur. P. Johnson's site opens playfully with a child's cartoon drawing and an invitation to 'Come on in!'. Inside, however, this is a rather sophisticated production, with a sleek, low-key feel and many extended pieces of serious writing on wine, as well as lots of tasting notes, wine recommendations and profiles of some prominent figures in the world of wine. Johnson's opinions are balanced and he clearly knows his wine. The writing style is casual but informed, and Johnson regains some of that opening screen's playfulness in his wine descriptions: 'This wine isn't quite so classy to start with and her voice starts to crack by the end of the evening, but in between she sings some very pretty notes.'

Navigation is rather good, with the consistent use of a navigation panel running down the left-hand side of each screen and repeated at the bottom of longer pages. Only one section of the site — the 'Photo Album' — breaks out into a different format, but a button takes you back to the main site.

SPECIAL FEATURES

Interviews The interviews are with top people in the wine industry: wine-makers, distributors and merchants. These are almost exclusively Americans, and occasionally the interviews dwell on topics — of local legislation, or geography — that are a little bit obscure for those of us outside the US. Otherwise these in-depth and revealing conversations with some fascinating characters make absorbing reading, and all are illustrated with good quality photographs.

Articles Several of the pieces collected here are not so much fully fledged articles as brief musings based around notes from themed wine tastings, such as 'Great White Wonders of 1999'. There are, however, several highly original and more thought-provoking pieces of writing. 'Johnson's Law of

Expectations' for example is a tongue-in-cheek look at the disappointments and delights of the wine drinker. Johnson's basic formula is 'P = 2R - E'. As he explains: 'P is Pleasure, R is Results and E is Expectation. So let's say you have a bottle of 1982 Margaux. Your Expectations are 96. Your Results are 86. But your actual Pleasure is only a measly 76, because it falls so short of your high expectations. Conversely, let's say you open a 1980 Clerc-Milon. Your Expectations are 79. Your Results, a very respectable 85. But your Pleasure, by my law, registers a lofty 91, because your expectations were so happily exceeded.'

Tasting Notes Johnson presents his notes chronologically, and as he says himself 'I realize this is a royal pain for folks simply seeking a recommendation for a good Chardonnay' so he also provides a search facility. His notes cover wines from around the globe and are reliable. Stars are awarded for each wine, and often a little bit of background information is provided as well as an orthodox tasting note.

Under $16 Obviously this would be a little more useful if the wines were all available in Britain, and British prices and stockists were quoted. Nevertheless, many of the wines are familiar names on British supermarket shelves and Johnson has a shrewd eye for a good wine deal. As he says, 'not just good for the money, but good, period.'

OTHER FEATURES

The Photo Album is a small gallery of images from California's wine country. These conjure up the sunshine and relaxed ambiance of the area, and some carry captions to put them in context. **Event Calendar** concerns itself with non-commercial events on the West Coast. **Wine Links** has in-depth profiles of several wine sites, plus links to many others.

A very well-designed and easy-to-use site, it strikes a good balance. As well as serious, expert scrutiny of wine and wine-making, there is much of more general interest, often with a sprinkling of irreverent humour.

www.winesenz.co.nz
Wine Sense

Overall rating:	★ ★ ★ ★		
Classification:	Enthusiasts	Readability:	★ ★ ★ ★ ★
Updating:	Frequently	Content:	★ ★ ★ ★
Navigation:	★ ★ ★ ★	Speed:	★ ★ ★

(NZ)

This attractively designed and easy-to-use site is a guide to tasting and enjoying wines. It bills itself as 'a sensual guide to wine', and whilst it may not quite live up to its sexy subtitle, it is indeed a celebration of wine enjoyment that encourages its visitors to get the most out of every glass by understanding more about wine and wine-tasting.

The author, Paul White, has a clear and concise writing style and is a gifted educator, befitting his experience as a wine writer, judge and buyer. His introductions to wine-tasting and wine appreciation are very readable and entertaining.

Other information is equally dependable. The site is basically a series of 'how to' guides with sensible, high-quality explanations. His phonetic pronunciation guide to wine grape names is a little erratic.

The site mimics the classic frames layout, with every screen featuring a navigation bar down the left-hand edge which offers links to all sections. Pages are long, so at the bottom of each page these links are repeated.

SPECIAL FEATURES

Tasting Guide A step-by-step tour of what to look out for when tasting and assessing a wine. It deals with concepts like aroma, flavour and texture, as well a particularly well-put together section on how to assess these components on the nose and palate. It teaches you how to identify tannins, acidity and quality of fruit.

Tasting technique Another very useful step-by-step section. Each stage of the formal wine-tasting process is introduced and explained, along with photographic illustrations.

Tips and Trends White tries to second-guess where we should be looking for the next big thing in wine in terms of regions, grape varieties and styles. More interesting however, is the second topic of this section, entitled Quick and Handy Tips. Here White simply lists a dozen Dos and Don'ts that form a neat and clever reference pack. For example, 'Do rinse wine glasses well, dry them upside down on a rack, and sniff before using', 'Don't over-fill glasses. The empty upper space helps develop aromas.'

Classic Styles Once complete this will be another star section, but for now only white and red wines are included, sweet, sparkling and fortified are missing. What's here is good however, with a thorough introduction to wine styles in terms of flavour, aging potential, and other characteristics. There are also links to numerous tasting notes, mostly of recent vintages from New Zealand.

OTHER FEATURES

Wine Flavours explains how different wine-making techniques affect flavour. **Food and Wine** doesn't go in for tables of suggested matches, but concentrates more on establishing guidelines and philosophies for this sometimes tricky area. **Practical Info** is just that: information on subjects such as choosing glassware, storing wine and decanting.

This is a fine reference source with a lot of very well-presented and high-quality information and advice. One of the best web-based resources for those wishing to make the leap from casual glugger to a deeper appreciation of wine.

www.wine-lovers-page.com/wineguest/wgg.html			
The Super Gigantic Winegrape Glossary			
Overall rating: ★ ★ ★			
Classification:	Enthusiasts	**Readability:**	★ ★ ★ ★ ★
Updating:	Infrequently	**Content:**	★ ★ ★ ★
Navigation:	★ ★ ★ ★	**Speed:**	★ ★
US			

This has to be one of the most profound and complete reference sites on the web. Anthony J. Hawkins presents an A-Z of wine grapes. Each entry fully describes the grape in terms of its history, where it is grown and the styles of wine made from it. The site is basically one huge, long page (almost 400kb in size, so at standard modem speeds allow at least two minutes to load fully). Once it is loaded, however, it is really very fast and flexible to use. It will also print onto about 160 pages if you wish to make a hard copy.

SPECIAL FEATURES

Grape Glossary is what the site is all about and in fact there is not one, but three of these:

Vitis Vinifera is the wine grape. Vitis vinifera varieties are all the biggies such as Chardonnay, and Cabernet Sauvignon that dominate the international wine-making world. As far as making wine is concerned, these are the aristocrats of the grape world. For each Hawkins provides notes on cultivation of the variety, a description of its characteristics and any synonyms by which it is known in different countries.

Lesser/Crossed Vinifera Varieties includes more obscure varieties that you are unlikely to find bottled on your supermarket shelf ('make mine an Albalonga'), as well as cross-breeds. Crosses are very important in certain wine-producing countries like Germany, where the grapes have been specially developed to ripen early in an often marginal climate. This section contains many hundreds of entries.

French-American/AmericanHybrid/NativeVarieties lists those vines that are non-Vinifera species. Vitis labruscana for example, is a species quite common in North America. Wines made from grapes like Triumph, Vidal and Baco Noir are not uncommon, though rarely seen in Europe.

OTHER FEATURES

Hybrids contains general information on cross-breeds, including the origin and reason for development of particular crosses.

Links to a small number of sites which contain high quality images of either wine grape varieties or pests.

Whilst of fairly specialised interest, this site is a terrific resource for anyone with general questions about grapes, or who has ever wondered about that unusual bottle picked up on a foreign holiday. The massive file size requires a little patience when downloading, but the quality of content, cross-referencing and thoroughness is entirely commendable.

www.wineplace.nu
The Wine Place

Overall rating:	★★★		
Classification:	Enthusiasts	Readability:	★★★★
Updating:	Frequently	Content:	★★★
Navigation:	★★★★	Speed:	★★★★★
SIN			

Author Simon Tan is a wine enthusiast who has expanded and improved his site continually over the past couple of years. It features a host of good quality educational material and has built into a significant resource with more substantial articles than in many wines sites. Tan's use of English is occasionally a little stilted, but that's nit-picking, since it's as good as many first-language English writers on the web! His meaning is always clear and it is easy to understand and enjoy his essays and special features.

In general the large amount of educational material here is good, detailed and accurate. I would quibble over some sections which tend to over-simplify. I also wouldn't put too much faith in Tan's Pronunciation Guide, a phonetic rendering of tricky wine terms that contains many glaring errors.

Load speeds are very good. The site uses simple frames with a navigation bar always visible down the left-hand edge of the screen, which links to all the site's sub-sections.

SPECIAL FEATURES

Wine Parties A concise and useful guide to throwing your own wine-tasting event. All the practical arrangements are dealt with and Tan suggests five specific formats with detailed instructions and advice.

Red Wines/White Wines These two sections offer a very comprehensive guide to styles of wine, and why they are all so different. It breaks wines down in to categories ('Light-bodied reds', 'Crisp un-oaked whites') and gives examples of each. All major grape varieties are listed along with their typical characteristics, and finally, there's a handy reference to classic Old World wines and what grape varieties lie behind names like Bordeaux, Burgundy or Rioja.

Health effects A very detailed and informative rundown on the links between health and wine. The emphasis is on the positive aspects, from reducing the likelihood of migraine headaches (an enzyme called PST-P does the trick apparently) to helping ward-off cold-sores (this time it's the polyphenols). It would have been more helpful had sources been given for some of the claims.

OTHER FEATURES

Tasting, Serving and **Storage** Excellent reference sections, which are extremely detailed and well put together, with temperature charts, tables of wine storage suppliers, and a host of facts and figures.

Wine Articles is a collection of essays and special features written by Tan and various other contributors.

Wine Quotes is a huge section, broken down into several categories inluding Biblical, Movies and Love of Wine which contain sometimes witty, sometimes profound and often amusing sayings about wine.

There's also a section of the site devoted to local Singaporean wine events and news.

A fine set of educational resources presented clearly and concisely. The site is exceptionally easy to use and contains lots of well-researched information.

www.geocities.com/winelabels/			
Unusual Wines			
Overall rating: ★★★			
Classification: Enthusiasts		**Readability:**	★★★
Updating:	Weekly	**Content:**	★★★★
Navigation:	★★★★	**Speed:**	★★★
(UK)			

This site celebrates diversity, looking at wines that break the mould in some way. It is of limited usefulness perhaps, but is diverting and lots of fun. The large, bold font used is clear, but makes scanning larger text areas slightly difficult. The writing style is unpretentious and factual, often concerned with the people and stories behind a wine rather than the wine itself.

Clearly, author Peter May has a passion for the quirky and unusual in wine, and there are detailed facts on some pretty obscure examples; so obscure I defy most people to argue with his authority on these subjects — I certainly won't!

There is a handful of sections to the site, and each of them features a colourful navigation panel with links to all sections. It is situated at the bottom right of every page.

SPECIAL FEATURES

Unusual Labels Scores of fascinating and often amusing labels from around the world, most submitted by visitors. Look out for 'Marilyn Merlot', or 'Fat Bastard Chardonnay', or even 'Cat's Pee on a Gooseberry Bush!' May often includes the story behind these quirky labels, making this section a unique and very entertaining place on the web.

Unusual Varietals No Chardonnays or Cabernets in evidence here as May introduces us to the delights of the Xinomavro from Greece or the Kékfrankos from Hungary. May gives some idea of what they taste like, as well as some serious viticultural background information.

Unusual Wines Some wines that are unusual in other ways. Here you will find some thought-provoking and surprising entries, such as the 'Fair Valley' Chenin Blanc from South Africa, a winery run as a political experiment with mutual ownership and profit-sharing amongst the workers. How about 'The Cataclysm,' a wine made in California from grapes harvested on 17 October 1989: the day of the San Francisco earthquake...?

OTHER FEATURES

Unusual Places is a small selection of wines made in trying conditions; like Château Musar from the war-ravaged Bekaa Valley (see p.107),or 'Africus Rex' made in a small garden in cold, rainy Ontario, Canada. There is a small selection of links to other wine appreciation sites.

Up against the hundreds of wine sites out there in cyberspace, Unusual Wine's ace in the pack is its unique subject matter allied to a terrific sense of fun. Don't come here for an all-round wine education or extensive library of tasting notes, but just to marvel at some of the most strange and outrageous products the wine world has to offer.

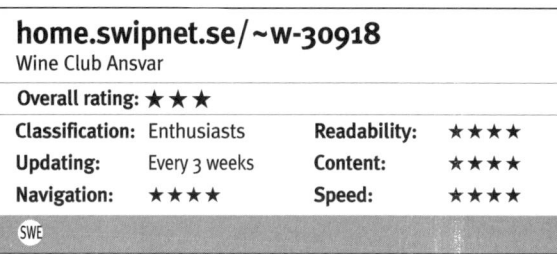

home.swipnet.se/~w-30918			
Wine Club Ansvar			
Overall rating: ★★★			
Classification:	Enthusiasts	Readability:	★★★★
Updating:	Every 3 weeks	Content:	★★★★
Navigation:	★★★★	Speed:	★★★★
SWE			

This long-established site belongs to a group of wine-crazy Swedes, known as The Ansvar Tasting Group. In it you will find a vast collection of tasting notes going back to 1981, but not a lot else. The range and quality of the notes earns it a place in this book, however. The quality of written English is very good, the occasional oddity quite charming. The tasting notes are clear and concise.

The tasting notes are very consistent and full information is given on each wine, including price in kronor. I found the opinions expressed here to be very reliable.

Most pages are text-only so load speeds are good. The site uses simple frames with a navigation bar always visible down the left-hand edge of the screen linking to all the site's sub-sections.

SPECIAL FEATURES

Tasting Notes, 1995—2000 This is what the site is all about, with literally thousands of tasting notes presented in chronological order. The group scores each wine out of 20, and they usually have a theme for each tasting, such as 'The wines of Greece', and 'Chardonnay: Old World vs. New'. Everything is tasted, from everyday wines to the fine and rare. Often there's a summing-up of the tasting in the form of general commentary on the style of wine or region being featured.

Gallery What a jolly lot these Scandinavians are. Photos of the Ansvar club, all having a very good time and sporting a nifty line in Hawaiian shirts!

There's something very friendly and welcoming about this site that makes it worth a few minutes of your cyber-time. The repository of notes is useful and reliable and there's something on every page for a wine-nut to mull over.

www.maths.ed.ac.uk/people/tnb/wine			
Toby Bailey's Tasting Notes			
Overall rating: ★ ★ ★			
Classification:	Enthusiasts	**Readability:**	★ ★ ★ ★
Updating:	Weekly	**Content:**	★ ★ ★ ★ ★
Navigation:	★	**Speed:**	★ ★ ★ ★ ★
UK			

Toby Bailey and his brother Richard are academics at Edinburgh and Oxford Universities respectively, who share an obvious knowledge and passion for wine. This site is really nothing more than a massive collection of several thousand tasting notes which are succinct to the point of being abrupt. This is no-nonsense stuff that comments on each wine in a direct, terse but very knowledgeable style.

The site scores well in two areas: sheer volume and reliability of information. The brothers taste a phenomenal amount of wine and their notes seem very reliable.

On the other hand the site scores badly for navigation because finding a note on a specific wine is extremely difficult. If you want a tasting note for the 1967 Château Lafite, it's there alright, but scrolling through thousands of chronological notes to find it is the only way. That's a tedious chore. The site is crying out for a decent search facility.

You enter the site via the Current Notes page. There is a link to Previous Months which takes you to an index of historical tasting notes. This in turn has a link back to Current Notes at the bottom of the page. Load speeds are excellent due to the simplicity of the pages.

SPECIAL FEATURES

Tasting Notes Current tasting notes are listed in reverse chronological order on the home page. Previous Notes presents links to thousands of notes grouped by year, and then month, going back to September 1995. For each wine a comment and score out of 100 is included. Suppliers are given where known, as well as prices at the time of writing. The Bailey brothers drink and taste a lot good stuff so the notes cover everything from ancient and rare clarets to the most interesting wines of the New World. Only very rarely do they venture outside the fine wine area into more mundane bottles.

Edinburgh Restaurant Guide This is tricky to find, and only linked from Toby Bailey's main page, not the wine page: (www.maths.ed.ac.uk/people/tnb). It is a very useful guide to the Scottish Capital's dining scene, from Michelin-starred luxury, to cheap and cheerful vegetarian. Detailed critiques are offered, with addresses and phone numbers.

The tasting note data collected in this site is worthy of any wine-lovers' attention. This volume and quality of notes is a rare find on the web. Whether or not you'll be willing to put up with the frustrations of poor search capabilities and rather clunky navigation is another matter, but you, like me, might get hooked by this short and snappy rundown on what the brothers are drinking. I find myself checking in for five minutes every week and there is always something new to catch up on.

www.christophs.org			
Christoph's Quarterly			
Overall rating: ★ ★ ★			
Classification:	Enthusiasts	Readability:	★★★★
Updating:	Weekly	Content:	★★★
Navigation:	★★★★	Speed:	★★★★
US			

Justin Christoph is wine critic for The Philadelphia Sun, and the author of this site, which covers not only wine, but also art and cigars. It is a rather curious blend of reference material and philosophical ramblings on wine, life and the Universe in general. There's also more mundane, but possibly useful collections of tasting notes, reference data and essays on wine.

Quite what you make of Christoph's florid prose style will depend on what you are looking for in your wine writing. I quote: 'By opening a bottle of wine and giving it expression in my unique circumstances; however less than a projected ideal, I recreate the winemaker's art as a reader gives voice and life to a dead poet's verse'. The site is worth a visit for a giggle and for the Pseud's Corner value, if nothing else.

Despite the extravagant writing style, the authors and contributors are not elitist about the wines they taste and review: tastings range from a $4 Argentinian Sauvignon Blanc, to a $140 Bordeaux.

Christoph clearly knows about wine and lots of his advice, views and tasting notes are well-considered. There's also a lack of attention to detail occasionally, however, like a total disregard for diacritics such as French acutes and German umlauts.

It's not an especially attractive looking site. The background wallpapers tend to be in dark blues and blacks, with garishly coloured text on top, which is not conducive to reading the screen.

At the top of every page is a navigation centre with links to the site's main sections. Load speeds are pretty good considering the heavyweight use of graphics on some pages.

SPECIAL FEATURES

Wine Reviews Christoph has no truck with boring old tasting notes. Instead we get mini-essays wrapped around the wines being tasted. Sometimes the thrust is historical, so for example a tasting of German wines from the Pfalz begins with a detailed story of wine-making in the region. At other times Christoph uses the tasting as a springboard for his philosophical musings on wine as an almost mystical experience.

Wine Quiz A wine quiz with some tricky questions. It's multiple choice, and having chosen your answer to each question, a click on the 'Christoph says...' button brings up the answer and takes you on to the next challenge.

Reference Some useful stuff in here such as the Ullage Chart. Ullage is a technical term for the level of fill within a bottle of wine. Old wines always lose a little liquid through evaporation, this chart lets you assess if an older bottle has an appropriate level of ullage for its age. Bottle Sizes is a handy reference for the measurements actually contained in all sizes of wine bottle, from a Split (quarter bottle) to Rehoboams, Balthazars and Nebuchadnezzars.

OTHER FEATURES

There are vintage charts for France and Germany, a decent set of categorised wine links and cocktail recipes, cigar reviews and — nothing at all to do with wine — an Art Gallery of famous paintings.

A real oddity this. Christoph seamlessly blends existentialism, poetry, hard fact and impassioned opinion in a site that makes you wonder at times if he's for real! Surely worth a few minutes of your time?

---

www.wset.co.uk
The Wine and Spirit Education Trust

Overall rating: ★ ★ ★

Classification:	Enthusiasts	Readability:	★ ★ ★
Updating:	Occasionally	Content:	★ ★ ★
Navigation:	★ ★ ★ ★	Speed:	★ ★ ★ ★

UK

For the past 30 years the Wine & Spirit Education Trust (commonly referred to as WSET) has provided vocational training for the UK wine trade. Their various levels of qualification are accompanied by courses and a comprehensive syllabus. Recently they have focused more and more on opening these courses and qualifications to the wine-loving public, and to expanding their horizons outside the UK. Their site has a lot of information regarding these products and it is presented in a fairly dry and factual style, but it is clear and contains all the detail necessary for you to choose an appropriate course.

Much of the information on the site is fairly static, though there is a News and Events section which is mainly deployed in announcing WSET events.

Navigation is fairly straightforward and easy to use. Links to the site's half dozen main sections are provided at the top of every page. Within sub-sections, the bottom of the page also features a link back Home, and to the sub-section's main index page.

SPECIAL FEATURES

WSET School The school is one of the main sections of the site, and one of the main activities of the WSET. Here you will find all the detail you need to decide if one of WSET's training courses is of interest to you. You will also find timetables for all scheduled training courses in London, contact information for regional training centres and details of home-study options, including a newly launched CD-ROM-based version of the basic Certificate course. The opportunity to purchase materials or sign-up for courses is provided via on-line forms. These link to a secure server, so payment can safely be made by credit card.

News and Events   A whole range of tutored tastings, seminars and special public events is also organised by WSET, and dates and details of these can be accessed from the home page. Once again these can be booked online using secure server forms.

WSET Awards   This area of the site is for the WSET's corporate business, and the information here is aimed mostly at WSET tutors and those in the trade. However, it does include a directory of qualified Certificate and Higher Certificate tutors arranged by geographical location which might be handy if you are looking for a course in your area.

WSET Memorial Lecture   The entire text is given of the most recent lecture delivered by a luminary of the British wine scene. Past speakers have included Jancis Robinson MW and Hugh Johnson: no lightweights, and so the standard and entertainment value is high.

OTHER FEATURES
There is a links section, mainly to other professional wine bodies and colleges and some of the better wine information sites.

A nicely realised site that gives easy access to the information you need to find and book up for one of the WSET's courses or events.

---

wineserver.ucdavis.edu
University of California Davis

Overall rating: ★ ★ ★			
Classification:	Academic	**Readability:**	★ ★ ★ ★
Updating:	Varies	**Content:**	★ ★ ★ ★ ★
Navigation:	★ ★ ★	**Speed:**	★ ★ ★ ★

(US)

UC Davis' Department of Viticulture & Enology is one of the world's leading academic centres for wine-making. They are hugely influential, not only on the Californian scene, but throughout the wine-making world. As well as a mass of excellent academic and research material, there is quite a bit here to entertain and inform the amateur wine-maker, and indeed, wine-lover. Surprisingly perhaps, the vast majority of the articles, press releases and courseware on offer here is written in very approachable layman's terms. Maybe it's that laid-back West Coast thing, but a very casual tone permeates even quite weighty subject matter. UC Davis' reputation is rock-solid however, so the information here can be trusted. In any case much of the content is far too scientific and learned for us to offer any argument!

Obviously this sprawling academic web site is the cumulative work of many hands and unfortunately in such circumstances, navigational inconsistencies are inevitable. On the home page a menu of navigational options appears down the left-hand side of the screen and is repeated at the bottom of the page. Within most sub-sections the same navigation bar ends each page, but unfortunately some sub-sections break this pattern, including one of the site's most interesting features, Professor Noble's Aroma Wheel. Still, it does offer a link back to the home page.

The site seems to be updated fairly frequently, though there's no set pattern to this. A good deal of the information takes the form of an ever-expanding archive of newsletters and reports, and the frequency of updates seems a little erratic.

You should be able to browse using any browser, version 2 or above. However, many items are '.pdf' files that must be downloaded and read or printed using Adobe Acrobat Reader, a free piece of software that is widely available. Thoughtfully, a download is available from the site, within the Home Winemaking section.

SPECIAL FEATURES

Wine & Grape Info This section of the site contains several of the best resources, as well as a disappointing number of broken links. However, the following make up for it:

The Aroma Wheel is the invention of Professor Anne Noble and has become one of the major teaching tools for wine educators worldwide. The Wheel is used to help students find the words to describe the aromas and flavours in a wine. It has very general terms located in the centre, and the most specific terms in the outer tier. Novice tasters often complain that they can't smell anything or think of a way to describe the aroma of wine. The Wheel helps train noses and brains to connect and quickly link terms with odours. A guide lets you learn precisely how to use the Wheel and you can order a plastic-coated copy for $7, though it is reproduced in many text books on wine. One nice feature of the site is that Professor Noble tells you how to reproduce faults in wines (to mimic Volatile Acidity add a few drops of nailpolish remover to a glass of wine). This could make an interesting evening with your wine-tasting friends!

Making Table Wine at Home The entire text of George M. and James T. Lapsley's book of the same name is available for free download chapter-by-chapter as Adobe Acrobat files.

Cutting Edge News A collection of press releases and newsletters issued by the Faculty. There is some fascinating stuff here, including Dr. Andrew Waterhouse's paper on 'Wine and Heart Disease' and Dr. Carole Meredith's work on 'The DNA Typing of Grape Cultivars' which throws up interesting news on how some of our favourite wine grapes developed. Both of these can be found under Faculty Research Programs.

OTHER FEATURES

Within the **Cutting Edge News** section, **Calendar of Events** details a programme of wine-related events which are open to the public. Many of these, like 'Rare Blends 2000 — A Celebration of the great combinations of wine, food, music, and people that make up the California wine industry' don't sound too dauntingly academic!

I'm sure the students at UC Davies (many of whom will become the most influential figures in Californian wine over coming generations) have the same gruelling timetable of lectures and dissertations as students of any other discipline. However, being a Davis scholar of Enology seems an attractive proposition based on the evidence of their web site.

www.wrathofgrapes.com
The Irish Wine Page

Overall rating: ★ ★ ★			
Classification:	Enthusiasts	**Readability:**	★ ★ ★ ★
Updating:	Monthly	**Content:**	★ ★ ★ ★
Navigation:	★ ★ ★ ★	**Speed:**	★ ★ ★ ★

(IRE)

No, the site is not about Irish wines (that would be a very small site surely?), but the collected wit and wisdom of a group of Dublin-based wine-loving friends. It bills itself as 'a resource for the Irish wine lover', but the bulk of information is relevant to oenophiles everywhere. There are a number of contributors to the site, as well as many pieces collected from a variety of publications, which means the quality of writing is variable, though in general remarkably high. The tone is down to earth and often light-hearted and many of the longer features make fascinating reading.

This site mimics frames, with the popular format of a navigation panel down the left-hand edge of the screen. This has links to the site's half dozen sections and the links are repeated at the bottom of the page in longer sections. A simple layout and minimal use of graphics ensures that load speeds are quick.

The site is updated at least monthly with the group's tasting notes, and other sections are added to on a fairly frequent basis.

SPECIAL FEATURES

The Tasting Resource An attempt to remove any stuffiness from the business of formal wine tasting. The rituals of wine tasting are examined and explained with an amused eye on the occasional pretentiousness of it all: 'Formal tasting is for consenting adults only, involving peering, swirling, sniffing, slurping, gargling, spitting and other noisy and unglamourous activities'. The advice on how to taste is pragmatic and reliable enough, and includes a glossary of useful words and a list of grapes and where to find them: Chablis is chardonnay; Sancerre is sauvignon blanc and so forth.

Tasting Notes A sizeable collection of notes from the monthly meetings of the Preamble Club in Dublin: a long-standing group of oenophiles which meets once a month to taste and discuss wine, as well as have fun. The notes go back to 1996 and are entertaining and informative. Prices and stockists for wines are quoted and the group awards between zero and three stars as a handy reference to each wine.

Features A rich collection of longer articles on aspects of wine, penned by the site's author or extracted from other publications. Subjects include Investing in Wine, Exploring Alsace, a historical explanation for wine bottle sizes and the origins of the Cabernet Sauvignon grape. There are also pieces of more localised interest, such as a piece on the wine and cheeses of Kinsale.

Quotes An amusing collection of wine quotations, from the true but anonymous 'Good wine ruins the purse; bad wine ruins the stomach' to the rather forbidding 'Some of the most dreadful mischiefs that afflict mankind proceed from wine; it is the cause of disease, quarrels, sedition, idleness, aversion to labor, and every species of domestic disorder.' (François de Salignac de la Mothe Fénelou 1651 — 1715).

There's a rebellious spirit of mischief and lack of snobbery about this site that is quite infectious. Having said that, these Dubliners know their stuff and obviously have a passion for both the subject and for spreading the good word about the joy and fun of wine. As a repository of good information and as an ongoing diary of the lives of some down-to-earth wine nuts, it is worth a visit.

www.gilbeys.ie			
Gilbeys			
Overall rating: ★★★			
Classification:	Wine Importer	Readability:	★★★★
Updating:	Rarely	Content:	★★★★
Navigation:	★★★	Speed:	★★★
IRE			

This is the web presence of a long-established wine importer based in Ireland. They do not sell directly to the public, so the site's inclusion here is on its merits as an information resource for the wine-lover, which — for a commercial web site — is substantial. Not many commercial sites provide such well-researched and well put-together collections of wine information, though naturally it is confined to wines, regions and producers represented by Gilbeys. Given the caveat that Gilbeys sells these wines, the information on wines and producers is sound. When advice is given — on foods to match the wines, or a wine's aging potential for example — it is very reliable.

At first the navigation system comes across as a bit of dog's dinner, but once you get used to the quirks, it is effective enough, if by no means intuitive. The colourful homepage is little more than a small piece of introductory text followed by a drop-down list box. This box appears somewhere on every page and contains links to the site's sub-sections. The naming of these is idiosyncratic: the homepage for example is referred to as 'The Grapevine'. The enigmatic 'World's best cellars' is in fact a substantial section of the site containing producer profiles, tasting notes and Gilbeys online newsletter. To get back to the homepage, from any part of the site, click on the grapevine icon in the corner of the page.

For the vast majority of the site, loading speeds are good. On some pages large photographic images take the file size up to 100 kilobytes or more (big!) and these take noticeably longer.

SPECIAL FEATURES

The Wine Challenge A beautifully illustrated, multiple choice wine quiz with five levels. To get to level five, you must answer three questions correctly at each stage. You get instant feedback on your answers as well as a running tally of your score. There is a hall of fame where winners' names are proudly displayed.

World's Best Cellars This section is introduced by an opening screen with links to four sub-sections: Wines, Tasting Notes, Newsletter and Stockists. Wines features a grid of over 30 wine producing firms with whom Gilbeys work. Clicking on any of these brings up an introduction to the producer's history, wines and region. Often these pen-pictures contain maps, label images and photographs that makes this feature both useful and entertaining. Tasting Notes, like those on the back labels of wine bottles, must be taken with a pinch of salt given that Gilbeys are trying to sell these products, but by and large they seem fair. Newsletter is an excellent section, let down by the fact that it appears to have fallen by the wayside: the most recent issue is Winter 1997. Nevertheless, the content of the newsletters is very good, that last issue containing amongst others, feature-length pieces on Wine, Weather & Climate, regional profiles of Burgundy and Italy, a nice piece on writing tasting notes, and a food & wine section.

OTHER FEATURES

The Vineyard contains links to the websites of Gilbeys' suppliers. This operates via a frames system. Close the frame to get back to Gilbeys' site.

Though not regularly updated, and obviously coming from a viewpoint biased towards producers they represent, Gilbeys' site contains lots to inform, and with their Wine Challenge, to entertain.

www.vinifera.demon.co.uk
Vinifera Wine Pages

Overall rating: ★ ★ ★			
Classification:	Enthusiasts	Readability:	★ ★ ★
Updating:	Occasionally	Content:	★ ★ ★ ★ ★
Navigation:	★ ★ ★ ★	Speed:	★ ★ ★

UK

Site author, Ken Inglis, explains that he has worked in the wine trade since 1985, but has only started to appreciate the qualities of fine wines more recently. He admits 'My palate is far from expert but I have endeavoured to write useful, informative notes'. This is a little disingenuous, as spending 15 minutes browsing through the site will convince you that Inglis certainly does know his stuff, and his notes seem consistent and very reliable compared with the many wines we have also tasted.

Unless reading tasting notes is your thing there is little here to entertain you. Having said that, if you are interested in a sizeable collection of full and considered notes on finer wines (mostly available on the UK high street), then this is your place. Inglis is an experienced taster who has worked in the wine trade for many years and his notes often include his advice on cellaring potential or serving temperatures.

Inglis uses frames to construct a very flexible navigational system. It takes a little getting used to but is highly effective. On the homepage, three buttons take you to Introduction, What's New and Links. Each of these simple pages has a single navigation button back to the homepage. Also on the homepage are buttons for tasting notes. The tasting notes pages divide the screen into two vertical frames: the left being an index of notes; the right displaying the notes themselves.

Somehow, moving between the site's main sections can be rather slow, with a pause before anything much appears to happen. Happily, once inside a sub-section (A-Z tasting notes for example) things seem to move much more briskly.

Updating is the only major drawback with the site. The addition of notes seems to be done in large batches, but very infrequently. Although the site is definitely still active, the What's New page suggests that sometimes months can pass between updates.

SPECIAL FEATURES

Tasting notes One of the main attractions of the very extensive body of tasting notes gathered here is the fact that the vast majority of the wines reviewed can be purchased on the UK high street, without recourse to specialist auctions or a second mortgage. Many of the notes stem from Inglis'

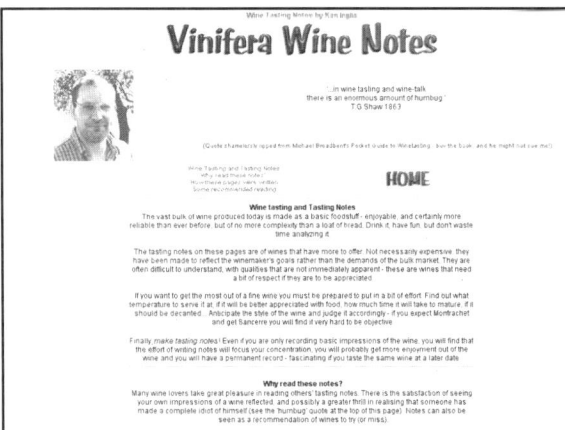

involvement in the wine trade, working for Oddbins amongst others. There is no search facility, though the database of notes can be queried in three useful ways: Tastings presents notes in reverse chronological order, with the newest notes at the top of the screen; A to Z presents notes in alphabetical order of producer's name; Origins presents the notes by country/region in alphabetical order. This flexibility means finding a note amongst the hundreds on the site is not too difficult.

Introduction From introducing himself and explaining a little about his credentials and his motivation for publishing Vinifera, Inglis' introductory page includes some further reading recommendations and a technical briefing on how the web site is put together.

OTHER FEATURES

There is a small **Links** section of a few web sites that Inglis recommends. There is also a link to the Malt Whisky Tastings web site of Gordon Muir. Nothing to do with wine of course, but the site is maintained and housed as part of Vinifera.

Ken Inglis has a direct, enthusiastic and very well-informed approach to wine that shines through in this site. If his promises to update more frequently can be realised then the site should become a regular stopping point for the online wine lover. Whether or not this happens, the repository of useful and reliable notes merits inclusion in this guide.

www.upenn.edu/museum/Wine/wineintro.html			
The Origins and Ancient History of Wine			
Overall rating: ★★★			
Classification:	Wine Importer	Readability:	★★★★★
Updating:	Rarely	Content:	★★★★★
Navigation:	★★★	Speed:	★★★★
US			

This academic site strikes a really good balance between scientific and historical detail, and telling the dramatic, human story of how and why the culture of wine making and wine drinking spread across the globe from its Middle Eastern origins. Illustrations are excellent.

You can't argue with the authority of this site. McGovern is a Senior Research Scientist who has published articles in Nature and Expedition on the archaeology of food and wine, and his book The Origins and Ancient History of Wine is the basis for this web site. Indeed, McGovern's discovery of one of the world's oldest wine jars, now listed in the Guinness World Book of Records, broke ground in the scientific understanding of how, when and where wine first developed.

The home page features a table of contents with links to about half a dozen chapters within. Beside the Intro button in Chapter One, you will see a small marker: this indicates your current location. When you click on any other chapter, the same table of contents will appear, with the current chapter indicated. Below is the content of the chapter. Scroll down to read the text. Often, links within the text will take you to other associated sections of the University's web site, but there are no return buttons; it is simply a matter of using your browser's Back button.

SPECIAL FEATURES

The Story of Wine is told in the site's first four sections: Living Out Our Past Through Wine; Château Hajji Firuz; Wine for the Afterlife and Under the Grape Arbours. The story is truly fascinating and well-told, with a sprinkling of humour and a lightness of touch that help explain the ancient origins of wine without the subject appearing at all dry. Photographs, diagrams and graphs are used effectively and all the really low-level scientific evidence is presented in separate pages, which you may or may not choose to visit. For example, Read About The Chemical Analysis is a sidebar to the story of the discovery of ancient wine jars. Take the link and you can see a Spectrum Analysis of the jars, and a mass of scientific data, if that's your sort of thing.

Map A colourful map of the middle and near East with symbols indicating the places where evidence has been found, both of wine grape growing, and of the storage jars which prove that wine was actually made from them.

Take the wine challenge is an interactive quiz that tests whether or not you have been paying attention! Your answers will be scored instantly. Just below this is a comments box, where you are invited to share your wine experiences: 'What's the best vintage you've ever tippled? the worst? Did you have good psychotropic effects? Or bad?' The entries from previous visitors are displayed just below and make for a diverting few moments of browsing. One participant, describing his time in the Sahara says: 'There was an unfamiliar wine served. Upon my inquiring as to its origin I was shocked to find out it was made entirely from fermented camel dung. The bouquet was unforgettable.' Yes...

OTHER FEATURES

Glossary covers not only some common wine terms, but most of the archaeological and scientific jargon used in the text. A Links page has connections to other wine and food archaeology sites, as well as a substantial selection of more general wine resources.

Credits lets you meet the team behind the research and gives you the opportunity to buy the complete story in the form of Dr McGovern's book.

That an academic institution and a learned team of researchers should present their work in such an open and enjoyable format is highly commendable. This site is well worth a visit if you are at all interested in the origins of wine. The story itself is quite absorbing, and it is told in a totally approachable and entertaining manner.

---

www.leskincaid.com
Les Kincaid's Lifestyles

Overall rating: ★★★			
Classification:	Enthusiasts	Readability:	★★★
Updating:	Frequently	Content:	★★★
Navigation:	★★★★	Speed:	★★★★

(US)

There's a bit of the glitzy showman about this site with lots of smiling photographs of your host, Las Vegas-based DJ Les Kincaid, articles like 'Serving Champagne — with Style!' and plugs for his local radio show. But don't let that fool you: the features on wine are well composed and full of valuable information. He illustrates each with photos or colourful graphics and often injects a dose of humour by way of anecdotes or amusing quotations. If I have any criticism it is that his style is rather stilted and overly-formal at times. Witness his explanation on how to open a bottle of fizz: 'It is prudent to place the mouth of the bottle nearest the first champagne glass to be filled in case the removal of the cork is mishandled and the wine begins to gush out of the bottle.'

This site encompasses Kincaid's triple passions of golf, food and wine. On the homepage some colourful oval buttons down the left-hand edge of the screen will take you into the section of the site dealing with each, which can be thought of as discrete sites. Within Wine, the entire contents are presented as a long list of articles which scrolls down the centre of the page, added to simply by slotting in new articles at the top. Click on any article and it is presented as a single page, with navigation back to the Wine index at the bottom of the page.

Just as there is something a trifle old-fashioned about the style, sometimes Kincaid's opinions are similarly textbookish and don't always agree with latest research (for example, his statement that 'it is clear that younger wines benefit most from decanting,' which at least one recent study disproved). But that is nit-picking, as the vast majority of the advice and opinion on offer is correct, sensible and reliable.

SPECIAL FEATURES

Restaurant Wine List Debockle (sic) Though a good spell-checker wouldn't go amiss, the article itself is far from a debacle, being full of rather good advice, like, 'Most wine lists are heavy on France's snob areas like Bordeaux and Burgundy, and the more famous wines of Italy. If your carte des vins offers multiple selections from a region such as Alsace, the Loire Valley, South Africa or Argentina, chances are that there is someone on the premises who genuinely appreciates these wines and would like you to enjoy them as well. Their prominent position is a message that the restaurant feels these wines go well with the house cuisine.'

Wine & Women Not, as you might expect, another of Mr Kincaid's Lifestyle passions, but a fascinating paper by Dr Phillip Norrie, a Sydney-based physician, into the particular risks run by women who abuse alcohol. Issues surrounding drink and pregnancy, breast feeding and breast cancer are examined (the jury is still out on the latter as to whether excessive drinking fractionally increases risk).

The Great Cork Controversy The humble cork is a very popular subject amongst wine writers on the web (and in print). Kincaid joins the fray with a fine essay that looks at the precursors of cork, and presents a full account of the historical reasons why the bark of the Quercus suber become the closure of choice for wine makers. The real focus of course is not on cork as such, but on corked wines: those that have been tainted by a compound in faulty corks. This essay looks at the statistics and the alternatives and tries to draw conclusions from the evidence on offer.

OTHER FEATURES

There are many, many more genuinely interesting articles in the list, dealing with all sorts of wine and wine-related issues. Other favourites include: **Serving Champagne With Style, How to Cellar and Serve Wine** and **Rating of Wines**. There is also a useful Links page. You may also consider signing up for **Les Kincaid's Lifestyles Newsletter** which will be emailed to you once a month with news on wine, food and golf.

Kincaid's site is one you'll probably either love or hate. The fact that the wine content is only one thread of the entire lifestyle package means that updates are irregular. There's also the question of his slightly pedantic writing style. Having said all that, there is such a significant body of interesting and useful work here that any wine lover will enjoy a visit and will no doubt find something worth printing off to enjoy with a glass or two.

OTHER SITES OF INTEREST

Daily Wine Review
www.dailywine.com
Going one better than several Wine of the Week sites in cyberspace, Nicholas J Noecker brings us one per day, plus archives (USA).

Gang of Pour
gangofpour.com
Lively site of a loose-knit group of friends and acquaintances based in the Metropolitan Detroit area.

Gidleigh Park
www.gidleigh.com
This is the web site of a superb country house hotel with an award-winnning wine list. Owner Paul Henderson puts the list on the web for your delectation.

John Gilman's Wine Vault
aoweb.com/jgilman
Lots of tasting notes on worldwide wines from a US enthusiast.

Pinotage Club
www.pinotage.org
Nuts about Pinotage, this site tells you what to buy, where to buy it and all about the wines.

Table Wine
www.tablewine.com
US site concentrating on affordable wines. Weekly wine recommendations and food and wine features.

Tim Whitcombe
www.ringsoft.demon.co.uk
UK enthusiasts site on his triple passions of coffee, music and wine.

West Coast Wine
www2.connectnet.com
San Diego-based, this is a large site mainly built around discussion groups, though the focus is decidedly on Californian and other US wines.

Wine and Spirit Association
www.wsa.org.uk
UK trade association's site has some public content, including some interesting articles and transcripts of speeches, as well as links.

Wine.com
www.wine.com
Slick commercial US site selling wine, but also with some good in-depth features.

Wine of the Week
www.nettivuori.com/weeklywine
Hannu Lehmusvuori is a Finnish wine lover with a poetic take on wine and an original site.

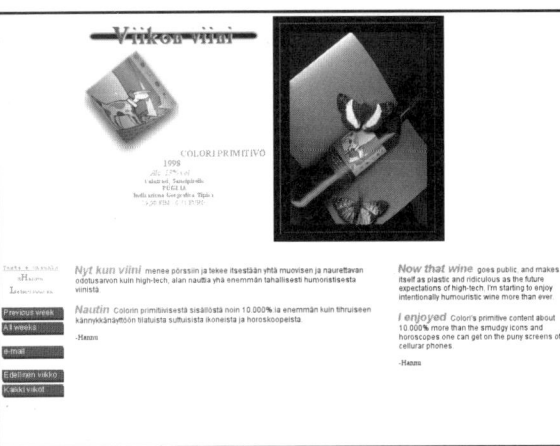

Winemaking Home Page
www.geocities.com/NapaValley/1172/
Rather clunky interface, but good information for the home vintner.

Wines of the Internet
www.anchorag.demon.co.uk/wines.htm
Horrible colours make this difficult to read, but it takes a unique look at wines the author Russell Whitworth has purchased from UK Internet retailers.

Section 02

buying and selling wine

Wine merchants in the UK were pretty quick off the starting blocks in terms of online selling. In a field where the USA usually sets the pace, the relatively compact nature of the UK wine trade kept them one step ahead. From seemingly staid traditional London merchants, to the swaggering young ecommerce start-ups, a whole raft of buying possibilities has been available to the British wine lover for several years.

Some pundits regard Web-only retailers with deep suspicion, proclaiming that shopping by wire must somehow lead to a second class service. It is true that on the Web there are no smiling assistants to understand the nuances of your likes and dislikes, but for many the whole concept of such a relationship with their wine merchant is an anachronism. Most of us will pick up a bottle or two from the supermarket shelf with our weekly shop, or are happy to buy from one of the many mail-order clubs.

With no expensive high street premises and no need to

hold shelves full of stock, it is hoped that the online retailers can offer options which are as well-priced as they are wide-ranging. Ideally, the cybermerchants will add value to the experience in terms of readily accessible information or interactive areas on their sites. Though this method of wine buying will never replace the relationship that many aficionados enjoy with their trusted merchant, there is surely a case for both to happily co-exist.

In this section we highlight some of the best online shopping, with everything on offer from vast portfolios of fine and rare wines, to cheap and cheerful selections that can be bought with the minimum of fuss.

www.madaboutwine.com
madaboutwine

Overall rating: ★★★★★			
Classification:	Merchant	Readability:	★★★★
Updating:	Regularly	Content:	★★★★★
Navigation:	★★★★★	Speed:	★★★★

UK R 🔒

Madaboutwine is the latest incarnation from pioneering on-line specialists Mark Bedini and Bud Cuchet who started up Fine and Rare Wines way back in 1995. They've learned that adding content to any website and not just commerce can generate loyal visitors. Uncorked is the site's reference section, and to give them their due, Madaboutwine have provided a lot of content such as food and wine matching suggestions and guides to wine regions. It has to be said that a lot of this information is rather simplistic and a good editor would surely have caught mistakes like confusing Portugal's Douro, with Spain's Duero. Background information on producers and wines is available.

The site mimics the filing cabinet look, with tabs for the site's sections across the top of the screen. When you click a tab the section becomes visible. Often there are extra links that appear within a section, which will also take you to another part of the site, but the tabs at the top will always indicate where you are. Always available on the left hand side is the Search Assistant where you can find wines using drop-down lists of category, price and style.

The search facility interrogates a database on your behalf to present a detailed list of matches. These are produced in groups of 20 at a time.

WHAT'S ON OFFER

The Wine List As might be expected from such experienced operators, this site has lots of tricks up its sleeve that make it one of the most comprehensive wine ecommerce sites around. There is a vast list, from everyday bottles to the rare and super-expensive. These are split between two sections: Wine Shop, where you'll find weekly specials and mixed tasting cases; and Rare Wine Cellar, where the esoteric and expensive are gathered. This site does have a vast choice of affordable wines which can be accessed using the Search Assistant. Though there are many thousands of wines available there is no option to browse everything within the Wine Shop (though there is within the more restricted rare wine section). The Search Assistant is powerful, allowing you to search by key word, category or price. There is also a More Choices? button which expands the search criteria to include region, vintage and food match. One very nice feature is that you can re-sort any list by clicking the button at the top to sort by Year, Producer, Region or Price (the default). Everyday wines start around £3.50, but if you'd prefer something a little more upmarket, £8,812.50 will secure you a single bottle of 1859 Mouton-Rothschild. Madaboutwine also have sections for buying beer, spirits and wine-related gifts.

The Service 'Never knowingly undersold!' is their slogan, and they promise a refund of 110 per cent of the difference if you can prove them wrong. They also offer a tailor-made Cellar Plan service as well as a Wedding List Plan. Faulty everyday wines will be refunded, but they state that they are not able to provide refunds for fine and rare wines which have been opened and prove to be faulty. This might be acceptable for older vintages, but since their rare wine list includes famous names from current vintages, I for one would challenge this policy if push came to shove. Delivery is guaranteed within five days to the UK Mainland. For all other locations it takes five working days from dispatch (subject to customs). Delivery charges are calculated for each individual order; orders over £50.00 in the UK are free.

Product Information Special selections and wines of the week are written-up in detail, otherwise the information is a little patchy. For some wines in their lists clicking on the name will display a label image and a brief tasting description. For many others this is unavailable and the click is wasted as the information displayed is identical to the wine list screen you've just come from.

The Ordering Process Every item offered for sale has an Add to Basket icon alongside. Each time you do so you'll see a running totals screen, with options to alter quantities and remove. You can then choose to Continue Shopping or go to the Checkout. Madaboutwine requires you to register before ordering online, so if you haven't previously done so you will now be prompted for name and address details, and to choose a password for future orders. Having done so you are taken to the order screen where you have to repeat this information. This is tedious, although you only have to do it on your first order. Click Continue and you will see a confirmation of your order including any delivery charges or discounts. Click on Next Step to go to the payment method and details screen.

More than the Hard Sell? Madaboutwine is a fantastically sophisticated Web site and business. A lot of the added value features on this site come at the price of supplying your e-mail address and name, which presumably fills their marketing department with joy. Having said that, there is a lot of freely accessible reference material. Under Uncorked you will find articles by well-known wine writers, beginner's guides to wine regions, grapes and pronunciation, and a food and wine section that has recipes as well as general advice. Easily the most comprehensive reference section amongst wine ecommerce sites.

www.wine-searcher.com
Winesearcher

Overall rating: ★★★★			
Classification:	Search Service	**Readability:**	★★★★
Updating:	Regularly	**Content:**	★★★★★
Navigation:	★★★	**Speed:**	★★★★

UK

Many people will use the site for little more than its single main purpose: searching for a wine and taking away the resulting stockist and pricing information. To do this is very easy indeed as the wine search form is dead-centre on the home page, and is repeated at the top of the search results page, allowing you to easily search again. However, there are a couple of other features to the site including wine links and book sales pages. Links to these appear at the foot of the homepage.

Load speeds are very good considering the site is driven by a very large database. It is clearly well designed and cleverly programmed to make the process as speedy as possible.

WHAT'S ON OFFER

Winesearcher is a very neat and extremely useful service. They have no wines for sale themselves, but can help solve the difficulties of finding stockists of particular fine wines. The service is free and easy to use, and claims to be the most powerful wine search available. Winesearcher signs up reputable fine wine dealers around the world who place their stock lists into Winesearcher's database. When the consumer comes along looking for a bottle of 1961 Château Latour, he or she simply types the name into Winesearcher, specifies the country and currency required, and awaits a list of all stockists together with price and contact details. If the stockist has a website, a link is provided. It is simple to see at a glance who stocks what, and wines are sorted by price (lowest first).

With around 150,000 wines in the database there is almost no fine wine that is unavailable. There's no doubt this represents a fantastic resource for the specialist wine lover or collector. Although obviously not all merchants are listed, it includes some of the biggest and most respected names in the business. Using Winesearcher you could save yourself a cool grand on a bottle of 100 year old Château d'Yquem. It returned three stockists, whose prices ranged from £1,700 to £2,550! On a more modest level, a test search on a decent 1995 claret produced several stockists and prices ranging from £33 to £47 — all for the same wine, in the UK.

OTHER FEATURES

Our merchants is a huge list of links to, and contact details for, the several hundred merchants worldwide who are on winesearcher's books. It's very handy if you're visiting New York and want to take in a little wine shopping, but also useful for finding UK specialist merchants.

Wine Books is nothing more than a list of recently published books with a direct link to buy the book from Amazon.

Fine Wine Links is a short but carefully selected list of sites, mostly of an educational and non-commercial nature with brief reviews.

As Internet retailing of wine continues to grow at a rapid pace, an unbiased facility like this is invaluable. Winesearcher can find and sort wines by location and price at the click of a button, potentially saving hours of research. The fact that it is so nicely executed and easy to use is a real bonus.

www.bbr.co.uk
Berry Brothers and Rudd

Overall rating: ★★★★			
Classification:	Merchant	Readability:	★★★★
Updating:	Regularly	Content:	★★★★★
Navigation:	★★★★	Speed:	★★★★

UK 🔒

Who would have thought that one of the most venerable and apparently staid English wine merchants would have been amongst the first on the cyberbandwagon? And the site is good, with an attractive interface and lots of useful information. Berry Brothers concentrates on upper-end fine wines, though not exclusively so, and there is a lot of reference material such as reports on the vintage conditions in all the main wine-producing regions. Clearly more time and effort goes into this useful background information than on many commercial sites and adds considerably to its appeal.

The top of the page features a Wine List Search facility where you can quickly home in on wines by country, vintage, price or keyword. Further down the page you will see a long panel on the right hand side that offers navigation to the site's main sub-sections. Within these, all screens have a navigation bar along the top: clicking the Berry Brothers logo takes you back to the home page, clicking the buttons takes you to the principal sub-sections.

Load speeds are good. The wine search facility presents a detailed list of matches with brief descriptive comments, but the whole thing is quite quick.

WHAT'S ON OFFER

The Wine List This fully database-driven site can be queried in very flexible ways, meaning it is easy to get to a particular wine or a selection of wines within your criteria. There are the usual fields such as country, grape variety and vintage, but you can also query the database by sweetness level, maturity, bottle size and price range. The latter offers a choice of pricing in Sterling, US Dollars or Japanese Yen. The site also has pre-set lists which you can browse such as 'Best Sellers' or 'Fine and Rare'. Berry Brothers' range runs the gamut of countries, styles and prices. As one of the longest-established names in the business their buying policy is tried and tested and the wines on offer are reliable. Prices range from around £4 per bottle (Berry's House White) up to several hundred pounds for rare vintages of classic wines. A selection of wine accessories and books is also offered for sale.

The Service A replacement or credit is offered on the return of faulty bottles. Where a wine is not to your personal taste unopened bottles can be exchanged. Older bottles of fine wine may well have some ullage (lowered fill level) and these will be marked as such and priced accordingly. Delivery is guaranteed within six working days (though there is a caveat that Northern Ireland and the Scottish Highlands may take a little longer). If your order is valued at over £250, next day delivery is guaranteed, and is also available on orders under £250 for a £12.50 charge. Berry Brothers also offer a storage facility: they will cellar full cases purchased from them for £6.60 per case per year. £7.50 is charged for delivery, orders over £100.00 are free within the UK.

Product Information The detailed information available on wines is one of the site's best features. For each entry in the table of wines, the left hand column has a link that brings up full product data, including tasting notes left by visitors to the site. Click on the producer's name and you'll see a short profile of the producer and a full listing of all their wines stocked by Berry Brothers.

The Ordering Process Quite a straightforward process. Alongside every wine is a small box where you can enter a quantity to select that wine for purchase. You must then click on Update Order at the bottom of the screen before moving on to another wine search. Each time you update your order you will see an order screen from which you can change quantities, delete items, or continue shopping. You also have the option to click on Complete Order. When you do so, you are taken into a secure server screen where a single form allows you to enter contact, delivery and payment details. It also confirms your order, including delivery charges if any. Once you are happy, click on Submit Order.

More than the Hard Sell? Alex's Wine Surgery is your chance to question Alex Murray, manager of Berry Brothers online store. Here you can send in any wine-related question and have Dr Alex answer it. You can also see the list of previously posted questions and answers such as 'Does putting a spoon in the top of a Champagne bottle really keep the bubbles in?' or 'How is it possible to make white wine from red grapes?' Wine News contains a lengthy and constantly updated list of news features. A comprehensive set of reports on the most recent vintages for the world's great wine regions is very useful and many of the pieces — on genetically modified wines for example — make for interesting reading. There are also good vintage charts and links to other wine sites.

www.bibendum.co.uk
Bibendum

Overall rating: ★★★★			
Classification:	Merchant	**Readability:**	★★★
Updating:	Occasionally	**Content:**	★★★★
Navigation:	★★★★	**Speed:**	★★★

UK

This colourful site has been recently overhauled and includes extensive information on producers, wines and regions. Pen-pictures are entertainingly written, as are the tasting notes. The information is brief, but good.

A frames layout is employed, with a navigation panel down the left hand edge of the screen that is constantly available. The bottom of each page has Back and Forward buttons, as well as a button to take you back to the top of the screen. Within the extensive wine list section, buttons at the top of each page link to the various categories of wine on offer.

WHAT'S ON OFFER

The Wine List Bibendum is a well-established London merchant with a classy portfolio of wines and a reputation for quality and service. They have a huge range, from the finest investment wines, to bottles that won't strain the bank balance: a happy blend of collectable rarities and more down-to-earth wines that fall into the everyday category. There's a simple keyword search just above the navigation buttons, and an advanced search facility within the wine list pages. Otherwise you can simply browse through the three lists: the regular Wine List, the Fine Wine List or Bibendum's *En Primeur* offerings. Within each list wines are divided by country and by region. Bibendum sells by the case only, though they list a per bottle price alongside the case price. Their range runs from around £45 per case for a French Vin de

Pays, all the way up to £3,000 plus for rare clarets. There is a tremendous depth to the range, and although all the famous classic fine wines are listed, the New World is well-represented with some of its hottest names.

The Service Only full unmixed cases may be ordered. All prices quoted are in bond and therefore exclude VAT and duty. Bibendum offers a wine storage service, and for a fee will store cases in optimum conditions. Delivery is free in the UK on orders over £100, otherwise it's £10 plus VAT.

Product Information Information is a little patchy, but where it exists it is of good quality, if a little brief. Within the wine lists you will find links to Region Info, Grower Info and Wine Info. Each of these pops up in a separate little window. Regional information is provided for only a minority of regions listed. There is more Grower information, and Wine Information (indicated by a colourful little icon against the name of the wine) is sometimes in the form of a tasting note, sometimes in terms of style and food-matching advice.

The Ordering Process This process is quite simple and fast. Against each wine is an Add to Order button which assumes one case unless you decide otherwise. Each time you select a wine, a pop-up Window displays your current order status with a running total, VAT and any delivery charges shown. There are options to Change Quantities, Go to Secure Checkout or Continue Shopping. Once you do go to the checkout a secure server page confirms your order and invites you to supply your name and address details (on your first order these are saved and you need only type a password in future). Press Proceed and you are taken to the final short page, which captures your credit card details.

More than the Hard Sell? The regional, grower and wine information is reasonably useful, but other than a news page used to announce Bibendum's tasting events, there isn't much added value in terms of information or entertainment.

www.bordeauxdirect.com
Bordeaux Direct

Overall rating: ★★★★			
Classification:	Merchant	**Readability:**	★★★★
Updating:	Quarterly	**Content:**	★★★★
Navigation:	★★★	**Speed:**	★★★★

UK

A long-established mail-order merchant that, along with sister operation The Sunday Times Wine Club, probably has more experience in direct selling of wines than any other operator on the Web. Though Tony Laithwaite did indeed start Bordeaux Direct driving vans full of wine from that region back to the UK, his company now stocks and sells wines from all over the globe, New World and Old, to a loyal UK customer base. You get the impression that Laithwaite really does believe in his products. His enthusiastic introductions to his regions, producers and wines and the reference sections of the site read well and offer some entertainment value in their own right. Each wine sold is illustrated with a high-quality photograph.

A navigation panel runs down the left hand edge of the screen and offers buttons for each of the site's main sections. This panel is available on every page in the site. Within sections, further navigational options are offered by buttons on the right hand side of the screen. This arrangement works very nicely, keeping movement within and between the main sections simple. On longer pages some navigation options at the bottom of the page would have been nice, but at it is you must scroll to the top of the screen to make a new choice.

thegoodwebguide 57

WHAT'S ON OFFER

The Wine List Wines available on the site can be browsed in three ways: by clicking on Hot Deals to see exclusive 'Web only' offers, by choosing Top 10 to see the current recommendations and finally by using the Search facility to find any of the 1,500 plus wines on the site. There are quite a few names here that are not familiar from the high street. In some operations that might be highly suspicious, but the whole philosophy of Bordeaux Direct is to source wines directly from the cellar door, and often they are the exclusive agent in this country. On the other hand, many popular producers are also in evidence for those that prefer to deal in familiar names. Prices range from around £50 to £150 for specially selected mixed cases, and from around £50 to around £2,000 for cases of individual wines (the latter being some very grand Bordeaux; the vast majority of cases are in the £50 - £75 region).

The Service A very fair and straightforward guarantee process is offered: 'If you don't like any wine, for whatever reason, we'll replace it. It's as simple as that.' Occasionally Bordeaux Direct will substitute wines for a later vintage or an alternative. They claim alternatives will always be of equal or greater value. However, if you do wish to receive alternatives you may select No Substitutes when ordering. They aim to deliver orders within a week, but ask for notification if your order does not arrive within 14 days. Orders are also welcomed on their Express Order phone line. The delivery charge is £4.99, no matter the size of the order, but is available in the UK only.

Product Information Product information is first class, with a photograph of every bottle and a complete style guide including cellaring and food matching advice, grape breakdown and tasting notes.

The Ordering Process This site uses the familiar shopping basket set up. The first time you click an Add to Basket button on each visit to the site you will be asked to login using a user-name and password. First-time customers must establish an account at this point, giving name and address details and choosing their login name and password. You will then see the current state of your shopping basket with options to change number of cases and a Remove from Order button against each item in your basket. Once you are ready, proceed to the checkout where you will be asked for delivery and payment details and shown the total price of your order including delivery. The whole process is pretty painless.

More than the Hard Sell? Bordeaux Direct scores well here. The News section includes very detailed reports from the wine regions written by Laithwaite or one of his specialist buyers. There's also a schedule of up-coming tasting events. All About Wine contains very personal but highly readable and entertaining guides to the world's wine regions. Beware; a small drop-down selection box appears bottom-left of the screen within this section offering the option of around 20 regions with full guides; this isn't obvious at first and I thought the section consisted of only 'Bordeaux' the first guide to appear. There are also excellent and amusing guides to grape varieties and wine and food matching, as well as Helpful Hints on choosing corkscrews and opening bottles.

www.chateauonline.co.uk
ChateauOnline

Overall rating:	★★★★		
Classification:	Merchant	Readability:	★★★★
Updating:	Regularly	Content:	★★★★
Navigation:	★★★	Speed:	★★★

UK 🔒

This French-controlled company is one the biggest on the Web. Their Unique Selling Point is sommelier Jean-Michel Deluc, formerly of the Paris Ritz hotel, who chooses and recommends their wines.

The crowded interface to ChateauOnline takes a little getting used to. On the opening screen a central panel displays the latest news and current special offers. In the right hand panel, beneath a photo of the estimable Sommelier, M.Deluc, are some drop-down lists containing his top recommendations of the moment and links to general information. To the left of the opening screen there are wine browsing and search options and, beneath, a navigation panel to several of the site's main sections.

The site is database-driven, but the load speeds are more than adequate, though a few seconds of blank screen seems to preceed the appearance of each page.

There is a good deal of information on this site, including quite a lot of topical features which add to its browsing appeal. Much of the background information to wines and regions is very obviously translated from the French. Whilst always readable, it is often inelegant and the translations are peppered with minor errors.

WHAT'S ON OFFER

The Wine List Over 800 lines are stocked, and there is a good mix with something to suit everyone from casual bibber to connoisseur. They feature wine from every corner of the globe, but being an Anglo-French concern, the line-up from France is extensive and is their particular strength. There are dozens of top quality Cru Classé Bordeaux for example, from the current vintage back to bottles from the 1950s. A clickable map of France lets you browse through different regions, with prices starting at around £4.50 per bottle. There are a number of special promotional offers at any given time, usually cases offered at a discount. You might just be interested in a bottle of rare port, believed to date from 1676, and yours for a cool £18,520. If you're an experimental wine drinker The Mix of the Month could be a good bet. It is a mixed case of wines from their tasting range and includes wines from several different regions. Taste-wise they try to include a bit of everything: red and white; sweet and dry; still and sparkling.

The Service Delivery is guaranteed within five working days for all promotional stock. The full range has a delivery guideline of one to three weeks. Chateau Online claim that every wine is between 5 per cent and 30 per cent cheaper from them than anywhere else and they offer a 'refund the difference' policy if you can prove otherwise. There is also a money-back guarantee if you are dissatisfied with any purchase. The delivery charge is £5.99 irrespective of size of order, or £11.50 for deliveries anywhere in Europe.

Product Information M. Deluc offers well-written notes on his wines that vividly convey the character of each. There's a description as well as suggested food matches, serving temperatures and advice on cellaring potential. Label images are featured for some wines.

The Ordering Process Against each product is a colourful little Add to Basket icon. When clicked, you do not see a confirmation screen, but the basket simply appears filled. Beside it is a Click Here to Order button. You can go on shopping from different screens at this point as in the background your order is accumulated, but at the top of every screen a Your Basket button will let you review what you've selected so far. When you are ready to purchase, click the Order button and you will see your order with the chance to alter quantities or remove items. Below are your payment options: phone, fax or online. If online, click on the credit-card icon. Previous customers can enter a login and password to save supplying address details, otherwise you will need to select Click Here If This Is Your First Order. Supply your address, delivery and billing details and click the Confirm Order button at the foot of the page. This takes you to a secure server area to supply card details.

More than the Hard Sell? The home page has topical features and the navigation panel to the left hand side of the home page offers access to several useful reference sections. Sommelier's Advice has a Weekly Wine Tips feature, articles on how to create a wine cellar and guides to wine-producing regions. Wine News is regularly updated with interesting articles including 'Brits conned by fake Rioja' and, believe it or not, 'Denmark, Sweden, and Ireland — The new wine-producing countries'.

A Monthly Column contains more features on wine and food. There are also interviews with personalities in the wine industry. The food features are satisfyingly meaty, covering the background and history of the featured food. They are accompanied by a small but well-chosen list of recipes which range from traditional to nouvelle cuisine and would more than satisfy the wine drinker who likes to rustle up a tasty dish to accompany their wine. With this in mind Chateau Online have thoughtfully included a recommended wine which is suited to each dish.

www.enjoyment.co.uk
Enjoyment

Overall rating: ★★★★			
Classification:	Merchant	**Readability:**	★★
Updating:	Frequently	**Content:**	★★
Navigation:	★★★★	**Speed:**	★★★

UK

Enjoyment is the online arm of the UK's biggest high street drinks retailer First Quench, whose familiar shop brands include Thresher, Victoria Wine and Bottoms Up. This over gimmicky site is new for Spring 2000, complete with animations and fancy Java tricks. They do, however, promise a standard discount of ten per cent off their normal high street prices, and offer a good selection of budget to mid-priced wines. Navigation is straightforward, via a little panel on the left of the home page that is always available. The site is colorful and friendly, making the shopping experience not at all intimidating.

WHAT'S ON OFFER

The Wine List The list is split into whites, reds and sparkling wines with a button for each in the navigation panel. For the large selection of reds and whites a world map is displayed, which you may click to select the wines of a country. Within the country list, wines are presented in alphabetical order of producer's name. This is useful if you are searching for a specific wine, but I'd imagine most visitors would prefer to see a list sorted by style or price. The wines on offer are mostly in the £4.00 to £7.00 range and include many familiar names. There are also some fine wine selections and an extensive range of Champagnes, prices for the latter rising to £100.00 plus for some rare bottles. There is also a collection of 'Star Offer' cases: with prices from around £30.00 to £150.00 for twelve bottles. These run the gamut from a mixed dozen of Spanish party wines, to a 'Connoisseurs Collection' containing some very smart wines from top regions and producers. All of these special offer cases are reduced by at least 15 per cent. Enjoyment will also deliver a choice of gift items, including hampers and flowers.

The Service Delivery can be 'expected' within five working days, at a fee of £4.99 for up to five cases. Charges for larger orders are calculated separately. Gift orders can be delivered on specific dates, every day of the year except Bank Holidays. Gifts can be delivered within two working days, including gift wrapping, for a charge of £6.99 per address. If a product ordered is not available at time of dispatch, enjoyment will send a substitute 'of equal or greater value.' You can return these within seven days for a full refund. If you buy a case of wine and find it cheaper elsewhere on the web within seven days, Enjoyment will refund the difference and give you an extra bottle for free.

Product Information For every wine listed, clicking on View Details reveals a nice product profile with a photograph of the bottle and a short tasting note. There's also a nice little feature where you can add your own note on the wine, which only you can see on return visits.

The Ordering Process Enjoyment requires you to register before you purchase a wine. Top right of the screen are little buttons for Log On and Register. For your first purchase choose register, and supply name and contact details. Having done so, some new buttons appear along the top of the screen which are used to check and proceed with your order. On subsequent visits, clicking Log On and supplying a valid password will get you to this point. Putting an order together is fairly straightforward. Whenever you view the details of a wine, there are buttons to add a case, or any number of bottles to your order. Each time you make a purchase, an order screen shows the current contents of your basket, with options to carry on shopping or Confirm Order. A simple confirmation screen allows you to enter an alternative address for delivery if you don't want the wines sent to your home account, and to supply a gift tag message if the wines are for someone else. Clicking 'Credit Card Details' takes you on to a secure server for payment details.

More Than The Hard Sell? There is a small selection of Web links to producers represented by Enjoyment. Other than that you are invited to 'email Serge', the cartoon sommelier who guides you around the site, if you require further information.

www.winebid.com			
Winebid			
Overall rating: ★★★★			
Classification:	Auction House	**Readability:**	★★★
Updating:	Fortnightly	**Content:**	★★★★
Navigation:	★★★★	**Speed:**	★★★★
UK 🔒			

Winebid is a US-based Internet-only wine auction house which has been trading since 1996. It launched its British wine auction arm in spring 2000, when it opened offices in Covent Garden, London. The opening screen features buttons for each of their auction sites: US, Australia and UK. Click on UK to browse or take part in the UK auction. Buying wines at the other auctions is possible, but beware high tax and shipping costs if you do! Buying wine at auction, whether terrestrial or real-life, will not appeal to everyone, but Winebid do make the process fairly straightforward, and the excitement levels of bidding and waiting in expectation are much the same as in the heat of the sale room. Winebid holds regular time-limited auctions, each running for around ten days. These might be the contents of a private cellar that has been put up for sale, or a miscellaneous collection from numerous different sellers.

WHAT'S ON OFFER

Buying Wines at Winebid For now all bids are in US dollars, so you need to work out a conversion rate before you bid. If the company is serious about its UK business, surely this must change? Remember too that like most auction houses, there is a buyer's premium to be paid on top of the hammer price. In this case it is 12.5 per cent on all purchases. The Provenance — a potted history of ownership and conditions of storage — is given for each lot, as well as a guide price and a reserve price.

Although you may browse the site quite freely, should you wish to bid you must register. The registration process is quite simple: you are asked to supply full contact information as well as valid credit card details via a secure server, although nothing is charged to the card until you buy some wine. Having registered you will be issued with a six digit ID number which is what you need to make subsequent bids. As you view wines, you can enter a bid via the bidding bar, or use Autobid. Autobid is a mechanism which allows you to specify the maximum price you will pay for a lot, and have the system automatically increase the bid in response to bids placed by others. For example, if you are willing to bid up to $75 for a lot that is currently at $45, your first bid will go in at the next increment, which is $50. If other bidders increase the bid, the system will automatically increase your bid up to your maximum.

Selling Wines at Winebid The seller's premium at Winebid is also 12.5% on all sales, so the company makes money at both ends of the deal. You submit a list of wines to Winebid for a free appraisal. If you are happy with Winebid's appraisal, you must send the wines to the London facility (Winebid can help arrange shipment). Once Winebid have received the wines, their inspectors will look at each bottle and generate the cataloguing information which will be provided at the auction. You will be assigned an account manager who will also provide a final appraisal taking into account the condition of each bottle. Winebid will also recommend a reserve price for each wine. Your wines will be incorporated into the next auction with space available. Settlement cheques are mailed 35 days after the close of the auction. Winebid claim that the vast majority of their wine is sold in its first auction, but any wine which does not sell is catalogued and sold in a subsequent auction.

OTHER FEATURES

Clicking the **Customer Service** tab reveals quite a bit of helpful information to guide you in how the buying and selling process works. The **Winebid FAQ** explains common terms that are used in the fine wine and auction world. For example, the term ullage is explained by clear diagrams.

Auctions are seen as one of the killer applications for the Internet: real-time information can be accessed from anywhere, bidding can be done from the comfort of your own home or office, and there's no need for the auction house to print expensive catalogues. Winebid seems like a tried and tested operation, with detailed information sufficient to answer any questions you may have. The mechanics of the auction are well-implemented and simple to use, but as with a traditional auction you still need to be knowlegeable and confident to purchase wisely.

---

www.wineorama.com
Wineorama

Overall rating: ★ ★ ★ ★			
Classification:	Merchant	**Readability:**	★ ★
Updating:	Infrequently	**Content:**	★ ★ ★
Navigation:	★ ★ ★ ★	**Speed:**	★ ★ ★ ★ ★

(UK) (R)

The real strength of Wineorama is its simplicity. Both in the design of the website, and the limited range on offer their aim is to make online wine buying as simple as possible. Consequently, there is little to read; tasting notes are confined to a single sentence.

Wineorama uses a simple frames layout, with a navigation panel down the left hand edge of the screen. At the bottom of this panel are buttons for White, Red, Sparkling, Mixed and Accessories. Each of these presents a short list of available products. Strangely, you cannot buy wine directly from these list pages, but must click on the Buy Wine button to go to an order screen where all the wine selections are repeated

WHAT'S ON OFFER

The Wine List They offer only a few dozen lines but these are from very carefully chosen producers. All wines must be bought in case quantities, apart from some specially put-together cases of mixed wines that are on offer at various price bands. Wineorama have chosen their wines well, with some fine producers and interesting and unusual wines that are far from run-of-the-mill. Prices range from around £45 to £100 per case.

The Service Standard delivery aims to be within three to five working days for all stock. Delivery costs £4.99 irrespective of the size of order (orders over £200 delivered free). Next day delivery is an extra-cost option. All orders are confirmed by e-mail and Wineorama will ask your advice if a wine is out of stock rather than simply substituting an alternative. You have 24 hours in which to notify Wineorama of damages for a full refund.

Product Information Minimal information on each wine, but the brief descriptive notes are accurate.

The Ordering Process The Buy Wine screen features a novel — if at first slightly confusing — arrangement where wines are selected from a panel on the right-hand side of the screen and details appear in a panel on the left. If you want a case of the wine, click the Add to Basket button and you'll see your order build up. You can remove an item at any time. Once your order is complete, click on Go to Checkout at the bottom of the screen.

More than the Hard Sell? Nothing to speak of. Wineorama will also sell you glassware, corkscrews and ice-buckets, but this is not the place for general wine information.

www.wine-owners.com
Wine-Owners.com

Overall rating: ★★★★			
Classification:	Club	Readability:	★★
Updating:	Regularly	Content:	★★★
Navigation:	★★★	Speed:	★★★★

UK

Wine-Owners.com is about putting buyers and sellers together for wine transactions. The site acts as catalogue and shop window, taking a cut of all sales. Sellers list their own wines by filling out onscreen forms which can include information such as tasting notes and condition report. The readability factor is pretty low therefore, especially as the process of getting to specific information is quite lengthy.

Getting the hang of how this service works takes a little doing, but once you understand the purpose of the site and the rules by which it operates, the navigation provided is pretty useable. Along the top of all main screens is a navigation panel with buttons for each of the main services provided by wine-owners.com such as Buy Wine and Sell Wine. At the bottom of all main screens is another navigation panel, linking to numerous other parts of the site, mostly reference and admin sections.

WHAT'S ON OFFER

Join Up You may browse around the site checking what wines are for sale without registering. However, if you wish to either sell wines or purchase wines, you must register. The process is relatively straightforward, and doesn't appear to request an excessive amount of personal information. You can choose whether or not to check a box authorising wine-owners.com to contact you if they feel there is new information that will be of interest.

My Wine Cellar Having established your account you may record your own wines in your personal cellar space. An on-screen form has various fields for detailing the wine: Wine type; Wine category; Grower; Region; Vineyard; Year, and so on. Some of these have drop-down lists from which you can choose, but it is still a long-winded process. In theory this service is offered simply as a facility to members, whether their wines are for sale, or simply for them to use as a computerised cellar book. If wine-owners.com genuinely wanted to provide such a service for owners with substantial cellars they would surely allow input via file-transfer, rather than this tedious typing chore? After each wine's details are entered, a confirmation screen appears which also has an Offer for Sale? button. If you choose to offer the wine you fill in additional fields such as price and quantity. Otherwise your wine will not appear in any list, but will only be viewable by you, using your membership password. This service does allow you to log and update your wine cellar free of charge, but the rather cumbersome mechanism means it is really better suited to what is obviously its true purpose: posting information of wines you wish to sell.

Buy Wine This section offers a search facility where potential buyers can be matched up with sellers who have wines that fit their criteria. A simple search box is useful for general searches, but for more specific searches there is the option of Advanced Search, which allows you to enquire about subjects like vintage, producer and price. The list that is produced shows basic details of all wines for sale. By clicking on a wine you see the description provided by the seller. This also tells you the category of the seller (Private, Trade or Merchant). A button marked Buy this Wine will initiate a contact with the seller. You do not make direct contact, but wine-owners.com will act as go between. You now must sit back and await the seller contacting you: the onus is always on the seller to make contact; there's nothing you can do if they choose not to do so.

From then on the transaction is between the two parties: wine-owners.com are now out of the loop other than receiving a five per cent commission from the seller. Note that this is not an e-commerce site, and the actual transaction is arranged quite independently of wine-owners.com.

Bid For Wine Here the seller can elect to make the very basic details of wines in their cellar viewable, but not actually priced and for sale. This allows bidders to make an offer at any time, which obviously the seller may accept or decline.

OTHER FEATURES

Wine Reviews lets you look up critics' wine review summaries that members have entered along with their wines. You can also add review summaries to wines you are interested in for everyone else to share, even if the wine in question is not in your cellar. Tasting Notes allows you to read what other members think about wines you are interested in. You can play the critic too, by adding a tasting note against a wine in your own cellar.

More than the Hard Sell? There is not a lot of extra information available at present, although wine-owners.com suggest they will introduce resource pages of wine links and a wine events calendar, in the future.

Though wine-owners.com launched its service charging only a five per cent fee to the seller of the wine (with a £5 minimum), their terms and conditions are full of caveats reserving the right to charge other fees in future: not only a buyer's commission, but fees for simply recording your wines. They also reserve the right to turn the whole site into a subscription-only service.

www.gotogifts.co.uk/for/finewine			
The Antique Wine Company			
Overall rating: ★ ★ ★			
Classification:	Merchant	Readability:	★ ★ ★
Updating:	Rarely	Content:	★ ★ ★
Navigation:	★ ★	Speed:	★ ★ ★ ★
UK			

The Antique Wine Company is part of an online shopping centre called Gift Ideas. The company has premises in Norfolk and London where their cellars hold over 10,000 bottles of aged wine, dating as far back as 1811, in carefully controlled conditions of temperature, light and humidity.

Mostly the pitch of this site is based purely on selling, so much of the text is made up of glowing reviews and recommendations. The few reference sections that there are such as vintage assessments are clearly and efficiently presented. Wine lists are filed according to vintage year.

In a frame down the left hand edge of the screen is a panel of navigation buttons, but these are for the different shops and areas within Gift Ideas and don't refer specifically to the Antique Wine Company. Navigation of the Antique Wine Company site is via half a dozen simple links towards the bottom of their homepage for each of their main sub-sections. Within these, a Home button is always featured at the bottom of a page, and sometimes links to other of the site's sub-sections. It's not the most elegant arrangement, but it is useable.

WHAT'S ON OFFER

The Wine List The Antique Wine Company's specialty is providing single bottles of aged wine for the gift market. Recently, for example, Paramount Pictures celebrated their Oscar awards for Titanic with wine from 1912 — the year of the fateful voyage — supplied from their cellars. This is not the place to come bargain shopping, however. The Antique Wine Company is in the luxury gift market. Wine prices are quoted including a hand-tooled birthday gift box, though you can deduct £95 per bottle if you choose not to have it. Even then, the prices are very high compared to what you would expect to pay from a merchant. The problem of course is finding these rare old vintages elsewhere. Also, the ability to purchase just a single bottle is not always possible at auction or through a broker. The list provided is an extensive sample of what is on offer, not the entire range available, about which you are invited to inquire. It is predominantly French, and predominantly claret. Vintages span from 1811 up to 1979 (the youngest vintage listed, though more recent wines are available on request). The Antique Wine Company claims to have established and verified the history of every bottle in its cellars, provenance being of utmost importance in such ancient wines. Nevertheless, there was a great deal of vagueness and inaccuracy in their lists: their 1971 Vouvray is apparently a red Burgundy, and I would hardly be inspired by a wine listed simply as '1955 Mâcon, Burgundy'. If you turn to the Antique Wine Company you are almost certainly looking for a special bottle for a very special occasion. For that, their range seems to be unequalled, but I would advise anyone considering purchasing such old wines to do some checking: make use of this site's Query Form to thoroughly check details and request a bottle condition report before ordering.

The Service The company are a little vague on delivery too, but state that you should be careful to put the date, if the wine is for a special occasion, such as a birthday or anniversary. They also state that due to the extreme rarity of the wines they are unable to replace them, should they be undrinkable, but are happy to send a complimentary bottle of champagne in its place.

Product Information There is basically no information on each wine other than name and price. Information on general vintage quality is available, as well as assurances about the company's storage conditions and the care with which they source their stock.

The Ordering Process This site uses the generic online ordering service for Gift Ideas. Against each wine is a box for entering number of bottles required. At the bottom of the current list are further boxes for you to elect not to choose the Gift Box or to downgrade to a standard box. There is also a button for you to Add to Basket. Each time you do, you will see a Shopping Basket Review of all the items you have chosen during the process. You may remove items, continue to shop, or click on Cashier to proceed to the checkout. All of your name, address and delivery details are taken on the next screen before you see an order confirmation screen with, at the bottom, a Secure Credit Card Payment button which takes you into the Secure Server area.

More than the Hard Sell? There is a brief rundown of every vintage back to 1900 in respect of the classic wine regions.

Maison de Pierre
www.maisondepierre.co.uk

Overall rating: ★★★			
Classification:	Merchant	**Readability:**	★★★
Updating:	Sporadically	**Content:**	★★★
Navigation:	★★★★	**Speed:**	★★★★

UK

Maison de Pierre is a small business, but one that has been trading successfully since 1980 under the stewardship of Adam Stonehouse. Stonehouse used to visit France every month in a large van, buying wines from both the traditional and the lesser-known areas, always dealing directly with the growers. The business has expanded greatly and they now stock a wide range from other areas of both Europe and the New World. Their stated aim remains to offer 'high-quality wines at sensible prices direct to our customers.' The website has been around for a while, but recently has been given an extensive overhaul as well as full ecommerce capabilities. It is attractive and easy to use with a clever navigation strategy that works well. This appears to be a very personalised service, and Stonehouse still counts his first customers from 20 years ago amongst his clients.

WHAT'S ON OFFER

The Wine List The good news is that Maison de Pierre offer almost all wines on the site at a substantial discount to their over-the-counter sales. France is still a stronghold, but there are also quality selections from Spain, Germany, Portugal and Australia. For those new to their service, the company offers special offer mixed cases, at substantial savings on the normal combined price. Single bottle prices start around £3.99 and rise to over £40.00 for some mature Burgundies and Bordeaux. There are some good if less well known producers here, such as Albert Bichot from France and R.F.

Buller & Son from Australia. There are also some fine Champagnes, including a giant Nebuchadnezzar of Champagne Joly (equivalent of 20 bottles) at a cool £835.00.

The Service Gift Packs are a specialty of the company. They will gift package any wines from their list, but also offer special sets of wines, beers and spirits packed with glasses, chocolates or smoked salmon for example. Maison de Pierre will organise free wine tastings to private individuals, small groups, private clubs and companies, presumably in the hope that you will place a juicy order or two. Delivery is free in Surrey, West Sussex, Berkshire, Wiltshire, Avon, Oxfordshire, South Bucks, Hertfordshire and Middlesex, or for five cases or more anywhere in the UK. Otherwise it's a whopping £16.75 for the first case, and £6.77 for subsequent cases, but for this you get an insured next day service with Amtrak.

Product Information There is a very good level of information provided. Click on the name of any wine in a list and a photograph will be displayed, along with full information on grapes, vintage, food matching suggestions and a tasting note. There is also a link to the producer's website if available.

The Ordering Process Beside each wine you may enter the number of bottles required and click Add to Basket. When you are ready to buy, click View Basket at the bottom of the screen. You will see your order, with buttons to Add Delivery if required, and to Buy Shopping. The latter option takes you into the secure server area for the entry of your personal and payment details.

More than the Hard Sell? In the small menu to the right hand side of the home page there is a Recipes button which will reveal a set of full recipes along with wine matching suggestions from Maison de Pierre's range. Growers, gives background information on several of the companies producers.

www.payneandrayner.co.uk
Payne and Rayner Wines

Overall rating: ★★★			
Classification:	Merchant	**Readability:**	★★★
Updating:	Infrequently	**Content:**	★★★
Navigation:	★★★★	**Speed:**	★★

UK 🔒

There's not a lot of browsing to be had on this business-like site. However, every wine listed is accompanied by the most comprehensive information to be seen from any online wine retailer.

All of the wines featured on the Payne & Rayner web site are exclusively available from UK agency Southern Wine Brands who have placed their total portfolio with the company. Many of these wines are not generally available on the high street, but only in the restaurant trade and are from producers of very good quality.

The site is simple and well-executed. A navigation panel is permanently available in a frame which runs down the left hand side of the screen. Lots of graphics are used to accentuate the attractive screens, which slows load speeds down a little.

WHAT'S ON OFFER

The Wine List Payne & Rayner carry only around 70 wines from a dozen or so producers, biased heavily towards the New World. Represented are some familiar names, such as Santa Carolina from Chile, and some that are not so well-known, but which are invariably rather good smaller-scale producers of high quality. Prices range from around £50 to over £200 per case. Clicking the Wine Cellar button displays a search window where you can enter criteria against Wine

Type, Country of Origin, Variety or Vintage, choose from drop-down lists. Alternatively, leaving each of these blank will display the entire list for you to browse through. One of the nicest things about P&R's list is the amount of general background and specific information available on their wines.

The Service Minimum order is one case, unmixed unless it is a special offer mixed-case put together by Payne & Rayner. Delivery is only during normal business hours, but the good news is that it should take only five days from stock. The Delivery charge is £10.00 per case, three or more cases free.

Product Information Against each wine is a Details button. Click this and a separate little Window pops up. In it you will find terrific details of the wine: not just a very thorough technical briefing on the wine and vintage, but tasting notes too, followed by a lengthy introduction to the producer, vineyards and regional information. In almost all cases there is also a link direct to the producer's website.

The Ordering Process Ordering is quite straightforward, if a touch long-winded. Against each wine is a checkbox for Number of Cases and a button for Order/Change. Each time the latter is clicked your order is added to and total updated (this can always be found at the end of the current list of wines being viewed). You can of course remove items by setting number of cases to zero. When you've chosen all your wines, click on Proceed to Checkout. You will see a confirmation screen and have a chance to alter your order, otherwise click on Proceed through Checkout. On this screen enter your contact details and delivery address if different, then click on the Continue button. A Comments screen is displayed where you are invited to supply some information on your wine preferences (presumably for P&R's marketing purposes) but this can be ignored by simply clicking another Continue button. There then appears another order and address confirmation screen with, at the bottom of the screen, a large Commence Transaction button which takes you to a secure online credit card screen. As I say, a trifle long-winded!

More than the Hard Sell? Other than their excellent product information which in itself has lots of interesting reference material, this site is very focused on one thing: selling wines!

www.theredandwhitewine.co.uk
Red and White Wine Company

Overall rating: ★★★			
Classification:	Merchant	**Readability:**	★★★★
Updating:	Sporadically	**Content:**	★★★
Navigation:	★★★★	**Speed:**	★★★★

UK 🔒

The Red and White Wine Co. isn't so much a company as a philosophy: they are basically a group of friends who enjoyed wine and who, as luck would have it, had contacts with some vineyard owners. Over dinner one evening they hatched a plan to identify and supply a small selection of Red and White Wines that most people could enjoy without needing the skills or finances of a wine connoisseur. This plan blossomed into the Red and White Wine Company. There's an infectious sense of enthusiasm about this small and highly personal operation. Their introduction to the company explains exactly where they are coming from, and from the detailed biographies and photographs of their producers it's clear that this is no faceless operation: the entire supply chain forms an extended Red and White family.

There's a navigation panel in a frame, which is permanently visible at the left hand side of the screen. Clicking on the buttons there will lead you to any of the site's sub-sections, which load quickly. There is no database behind their small wine catalogue, so the lists appear promptly, even though there are photographs of every wine on offer.

WHAT'S ON OFFER

The Wine List The extent of the range is not the attraction here: in fact, the wines of only two producers are imported, something like a dozen different wines in total. Each of these falls squarely into the moderately priced bracket, with several at around £5.00, going up to around £9.00 for their top-of-the range oak-aged French red. Despite the name of the company the list does include a rosé and a sweet white wine. Red and White are the exclusive distributors of these wines in the UK, so the names may not be familiar, but the quality is sound.

The Service Minimum order is one mixed case, but unmixed cases attract a 5% discount. They promise to do their utmost to contact you if a wine is out of stock, but will provide an alternative of equal value if this is not possible. Faulty bottles can be returned for a full refund. Delivery time is 10 days for credit card orders, up to 21 days for orders paid by cheque. Delivery costs £7.50 for one case, £10.00 for two cases, and is free for three or more cases.

Product Information There is very good product information. Apart from profiles of their producers and their wine-making philosophies, each wine has a tasting note, photograph and food matching suggestion, as well as advice on cellaring potential. There is also a selection of wine accessories like ice buckets and corkscrews, which again are illustrated with photographs and full information.

The Ordering Process Ordering is very straightforward. First of all name and contact details are entered, then wines selected from drop-down lists of unmixed cases followed by single bottles. Delivery charges are calculated automatically and shown at the bottom of the screen. Once you have chosen your payment method, clicking on Submit the Order takes you to a confirmation screen where the order and your details are displayed. If you have chosen to pay by credit card clicking Enter Credit Card Details takes you into Red and White's secure server area, otherwise payment by cheque or Bank Transfer can be completed by post/telephone.

More Than The Hard Sell? There's quite a bit of extra information on the Red and White website. **Other Websites** is a small selection of personally recommended wine links.

Wine Information (part of the Our Wines section) gives a run down on grape varieties, the wine laws of France and Germany, and advice on how to understand the information on wine labels. Within this section there is also a comprehensive and well-written glossary of wine terms, which covers everything from acetic acid to yeast. A technical description is provided for each entry, along with a few notes on how they relate to wine and the wine-making process and how they contribute to the character of the final product.

www.seckfordwines.co.uk
Seckford Wines

Overall rating: ★ ★ ★

Classification:	Merchant	**Readability:**	★ ★ ★
Updating:	Every 2 hours	**Content:**	★ ★ ★
Navigation:	★ ★ ★	**Speed:**	★ ★ ★ ★

UK

Seckford Wines, one of the largest UK stockists of fine and rare wine from around the world, was founded in 1981 by Chairman Richard Harvey-Jones. The wine list is indeed impressive, as is their grasp of the potential business advantages of the new electronic media: not only is the website attractive and user-friendly, but they claim their online stock list is updated every two hours.

A small navigation panel is located top-left of the homepage and on every main lower-level page on the site. It offers access to the site's main sub-sections, and includes a Speed Search Site box: a drop-down index of the site allowing instant access to specific pages. Some lower level pages don't have the navigation panel, but at least there is always a link back to home. Full details, sometimes a photograph of the label, and usually a tasting note pop up in a small window whenever the Info button on the wine list is clicked.

WHAT'S ON OFFER

The Wine List Seckford deal only in fine wines. They are strong in all areas, listing over 1,000 wines, some available in cases only, but also lots of odd bottles — handily, one of the search options is to retrieve only oddments if you are seeking just the odd special bottle. There's nothing much below £100 per case, and prices soar into the stratosphere at the top end of their list, but this is the collectible cream of the wine world.

The Service Seckford will try wherever possible to dispatch same day for all orders received before 2pm. Unless otherwise requested, UK orders will be dispatched via 48-hr courier.

Product Information Beside each wine in the wine list is a little Info symbol. Clicking opens up a separate little window with good information on each wine, including an independent tasting note by one of the world's best known authorities. These seem to be presented warts 'n all. For example one note by the writer Clive Coates on an old claret Seckford are selling says 'now past it' - and that was written in 1987! If the info symbol is coloured grey, there is no information available.

The Ordering Process Seckford is not yet a full e-commerce site. Instead, your order details are sent to Seckford by email and the order is completed by email, telephone or fax. Against each wine is an Order button. Click on this and a window pops up showing the wine and asking you to enter how many bottles/cases you require. Once you've done that, click on Continue and the pop-up window closes. At this point you can continue shopping, or go to the top or foot of the page where you will find an option to Complete order. The next screen captures name and address details, then Next brings up an order confirmation screen. Once satisfied, click on Next again and your order is sent by email.

More Than The Hard Sell? Not a lot of extra reference material here, though the wine information is useful in that it quotes opinions on the wines from the world's best-known critics.

OTHER SITES OF INTEREST

Amazon
www.amazon.co.uk
Amazon has a whole auction arm selling everything under the sun. Wines tend to be on offer from merchants as often as private buyers.

Cambridge Wine
www.cambridgewine.com
Independent fine wine merchant with a personalised service and terrific list.

Cave Cru Classé
www.cave-cru-classe.com
Headache-inducing site, but enormous list of the finest wines.

Chandos Deli
www.chandosdeli.com
West country food and wine specialist, with very strong Italian range. Full ecommerce site.

Classic Wines
www.classic-wines.co.uk
John Holmes runs this delightful small on-line merchant offering a limited list of fine, moderately priced wines. Personal service.

James Nicholson
www.jnwine.co.uk
Northern Ireland's shining wine star offering on-line trade from mid 2000. Highly recommended

Lay and Wheeler
www.layandwheeler.co.uk
Established high quality wine merchant, strong in fine wines but not exclusively so. En primeurs and public tastings. Full ecommerce site.

Laytons
www.laytons.co.uk
Small London chain with a range of fine wines and popular own-label Champagne.

Majestic Wine Warehouses
www.majestic.co.uk
UK's biggest case-only operation, but no sales on their website, just company information.

Noel Young Wines
www.nywines.co.uk
Another award winning operation with a terrific list and good prices. E-commerce promised in 2000.

Park Lane Champagne
www.parklanechampagne.co.uk
Company importing quality Champagnes and offering a personalised label service.

Peter Wylie Fine Wines
www.wyliefinewines.co.uk
Claret specialists based in Devon, en primeurs.

Raeburn Fine Wines
www.raeburnfinewines.com
Zubair Mohamed is undoubtedly one of the brightest talents amongst the UK's independent merchants and importers. Tireless in seeking out the finest wines, he deals in some wonderful smaller producers.

Sunday Times Wine Club
www.sundaytimeswineclub.co.uk
£10 joining fee, but lots of special offer cases, events and an extensive wine list.

Valvona and Crolla
www.valvonacrolla.co.uk
Multi-award winning Italian specialist based in Edinburgh, but shipping a superb range of Italian wines country wide. Full ecommerce site.

Wineraks
www.wineraks.co.uk
Scottish merchant strong in old claret, old vintages of Château Musar and more down to earth options.

Yapp Brothers
www.yapp.co.uk
One of the country's greatest proponents of Loire and Rhône wines. Specialised advice and service.

buying and selling at a glance

name of website	star rating	wine list
Madaboutwine www.madaboutwine.com	★★★★★	Mostly everyday wines from £3.50, plus some fine wines rising up to second-mortgage prices. Special mixed cases and promotional offers.
Winesearcher www.wine-searcher.com	★★★★★	This site searches hundreds of merchant lists. Hundreds of thousands of fine wines are accessible.
Berry Brothers and Rudd www.bbr.co.uk	★★★★	Well-known names, with prices starting at £4.00. Extensive fine wine selection and en Primeur offers.
Bibendum www.bibendum.co.uk	★★★★	By the case only. Classy portfolio from £45 to £3000 covering the globe. Fine wines and en Primeur.
Bordeauxdirect www.bordeauxdirect.co.uk	★★★★	1500 wines, many unfamiliar but from smaller producers of good quality. Most cases £50-£75, but fine wines costing into the thousands are also available.
Chateau Online www.chateauonline.co.uk	★★★★	Mostly French, but not exclusively, lots of special and seasonal offers. 800 wines from £4.50 a bottle.
Enjoyment www.enjoyment.co.uk	★★★★	Mostly wines in the £4.00 to £7.00 range, including many familiar names. 'Star Offer' cases have at least 15% discount.

service	delivery	more than the hard sell?
110% refund if you can buy cheaper. Cellar plan and wedding list options. Refund on faulty wines, but not on fine and rare.	Calculated individually, orders over £50.00 free.	Lots of good quality wine news, information and entertainment.
Searching for a stockist or best price on a wine? This service will list local stockists of a given wine by price.	Depends on the merchant you buy from.	Lots of good quality wine news, information and entertainment.
Unopened bottles can be exchanged if not to your taste. Storage facility for fine wines.	£7.50, orders over £100.00 free	Alex's Wine Surgery, vintage reports, charts and links.
Fine wine storage service.	£10 plus VAT, orders over £100 free.	Information on their own regions, growers and wines is useful. News page announces tastings events.
'If you don't like any wine, for whatever reason, we'll replace it.'	£4.99, no matter the size of order.	Detailed reports and entertaining guides to the wine regions, amusing guides to grapes and wine and food matching.
Refund the difference policy if you can find wines cheaper. Money back if dissatisfied with any purchase.	£5.99 irrespective of the size of order.	Weekly wine tips, regional guides and wine news. Plenty of food and wine matching guidance too.
Gift wrapping service. Find a wine cheaper and they will refund the difference and give you a bottle free.	£4.99 for up to five cases. Larger orders by arrangement.	Small selection of web links to their own producers.

buying and selling at a glance

name of website	star rating	wine list
Winebid www.winebid.com	★★★★	Auction site with an ever-changing set of wines on offer, exclusively fine and rare.
Wineorama www.wineorama.com	★★★★	Small is beautiful, with a few dozen wines from well-chosen producers. Prices from £45 to £100 per case.
Wine-Owners.com www.wine-owners.com	★★★★	Trading venue for merchants and public. Ever-changing selection of wines on offer. Seller pays a 5% commission.
The Antique Wine Company www.gotogifts.co.uk/for/finewine	★★★	Very expensive but exhaustive stock of vintages from 1811 to 1979 available. Aimed at the gift market.
Maison de Pierre www.maisondepierre.co.uk	★★★	Single bottle prices from £3.99 to over £40.00. France is strong, but also a small selection from around the world.
Payne & Rayner Wines www.payneandrayner.co.uk	★★★	Only 70 wines, biased heavily towards the New World. Good smaller-scale producers. Prices from £50 to £200 per case.
The Red and White Wine Company www.theredandwhitewine.co.uk	★★★	Hand imported and very small range from only two producers, £5.00 to £9.00 per bottle.
Seckford Wines www.seckfordwines.co.uk	★★★	1000 fine wines, some available by the case only. Lots of odd bottles. Nothing much below £100 per case.

service	delivery	more than the hard sell?
Buyer and seller each pay a 12.5% premium. For the seller, the company catalogues and estimates reserve values for your wines.	Not specified	There's lots of interesting background to how to buy and sell at auction.
Damages will be refunded up to 24 hours after delivery.	£4.99 per order, orders over £200 free.	None to speak of other than product information.
None. All transactions are between buyer and seller.	Arranged between buyer and seller.	Not a lot at present, although wine-owners.com suggest they will introduce resource pages in future.
If the bottle is faulty they are unable to offer replacements, due to the rarity of most of the wines. Complimentary Champagne offered in its place.	Included in price.	A run down of every vintage back to 1900 in respect of the classic wine regions.
Gift packs are a speciality. On site tastings for small groups and clubs are offered.	Free locally, otherwise £16.75 for first case, £6.77 per subsequent case for next day service.	Recipes with wine matching suggestions and background information on producers.
Special offer mixed cases from time to time.	£10.00 per case, three or more cases free.	Excellent product information which in itself has lots of interesting reference material.
5% discount on unmixed cases. Faulty bottles replaced.	£7.50 one case, £10 two cases, three or more cases free.	Recommended wine links, a run down on grape varieties, the wine laws of France and Germany, how to understand wine labels.
Same day dispatch via 48-hr courier.	£10 per consignment.	Not a lot. Opinions on wines for sale from the world's best known critics.

Chapter 3
regions

Britain has always been a significant importer and commercial centre for wines. Although France was the undisputed king of wine-producing countries, Britain enjoyed one of the most diverse ranges of wine available anywhere. To this day wine-making cultures have a much more parochial outlook on wine, and their shelves look very different from those of the average British merchant.

Twentieth-century developments in transport and technology mean the choice on offer today is wider than it has ever been. Wines from Mexico to Macedonia grace the shelves. The wine world has been on a rollercoaster ride over the past 30 years or so that has seen more changes than anyone would have dared predict in the sleepy decades that went before.

Thirty years ago was also a time of relative consumer ignorance. Almost without exception, fine wine was sold under the label of where it was made: Chablis; Sancerre; Bordeaux. Otherwise, catch-all brand names ruled: Hirondelle; Blue Nun; Mateus Rosé. What the casual drinker didn't know was what was in the bottle. The whole concept of naming the grape from which the wine is made is relatively new. So-called 'Varietal Labelling' has empowered the average wine drinker and given a simpler frame of reference: if we know we like Sauvignon Blanc we will happily pick and choose amongst Chile, New Zealand, Spain or South Africa. Ironically, some of France's old guard of fine Sauvignons Blanc — Sancerre, Pouilly-Fumé — are missing out on the action.

The resources pinpointed within this section will help you make sense of the global wine industry and will hopefully guide you towards even more informed choices.

---

www.wine.co.za
South African Wine Directory

Overall rating: ★ ★ ★ ★

Classification:	Commerce	Readability:	★ ★ ★ ★
Updating:	Frequently	Content:	★ ★ ★ ★
Navigation:	★ ★	Speed:	★ ★ ★

SA

There's a lot of reading in this site with a whole host of articles either re-printed from terrestrial magazines, or specially written for the Wine Directory. Many of these are to be found under the Wine News heading. There are also promotional advertorials, for example on the vineyards of Franchhoek, 'The French corner of the Cape', which although a puff for the region, does include an excellent primer on the place and the wines.

The directory listings for wines and wineries are very sound, and given that this site is in the business of promoting South African wine, the advice and information seems to be dependable.

The homepage presents topical articles in a magazine like format, with lots of news, special features and a diary of events listed in the body of the page. Down the left-hand edge of the screen is a navigation panel. There is another navigation bar featuring more or less identical options along the top edge of the screen. This latter bar is featured within most sub-section main screens. Other sub-sections have only a Home button, and once you are down at the level of the site's database of producers or wines, there are usually no navigational options other than hitting your browser's Back button.

The site is database-driven, and some results of searches do take a while to download: especially on pages like Wineries and Wines, where high-quality photographs mean large file sizes. It has to be said that the wait is usually worth it, but the best advice is to make your searches as specific as possible.

SPECIAL FEATURES

Wineries When first selected from the navigation bar this section displays a random winery profile in the body of the page. The means to access specific winery information is via the panel towards the left hand side. Here you can browse by region or by special categories like those wineries with disabled access or those that are open on Sundays. You can also use a search facility where entering the name of a winery will take you straight to its entry. These winery profiles are excellent. There is a photograph, a lovely introduction to the producer and their wines, full contact and visiting information and a full rundown on their wines including label images and technical data. You can even buy wines for shipping to the UK using full ecommerce facilities.

Wines Again a featured wine is shown to the right, but the main access is through the search panel on the left. Query the database by wine name, wine maker or grape variety. The result is a listing of wines with label images and technical data. Be warned: searching simply for a generic term like Chardonnay will result in a list of several hundred wines which will take forever to download.

Wine News is a collection of topical stories, many culled from other wine sites or print magazines. It deals mainly with issues of South African interest. 'My money for a glass of Pinotage' is the amusing tale of trying to defeat bureaucracy in a winery restaurant, 'Wine Wars — Episode One' tells the tale of the United States' complex and contentious wine shipping laws and 'Symptoms of a Wine Fanatic' is a handy self-diagnosis guide to see if you've got the bug.

Maps A handy section with a general map showing the main wine areas, individual area maps that get down to showing road numbers and the positions of wineries, and a wine route map that would be handy if you are planning a visit to the area.

OTHER FEATURES

There are some other resources here, such as a very comprehensive History of South African wine which also includes a description of the main wine regions and Noticeboard, a kind of classified ads section where you can leave a notice and contact details.

This consumer-orientated site sets a friendly and welcoming tone and does a very good job of introducing the country, its wines and tourism opportunities. Whether or not you are in the market for a visit there (one of the most scenic and easy-to-manage of all the world's wine touring areas) you will find this site delivers a good quality of useable information.

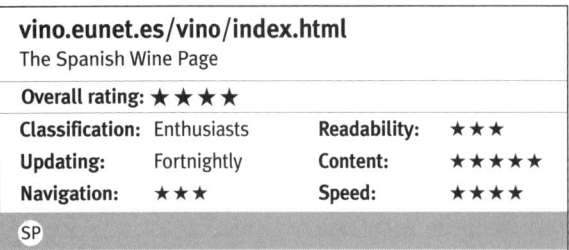

vino.eunet.es/vino/index.html			
The Spanish Wine Page			
Overall rating: ★★★★			
Classification:	Enthusiasts	**Readability:**	★★★
Updating:	Fortnightly	**Content:**	★★★★★
Navigation:	★★★	**Speed:**	★★★★
SP			

The stated aim of The Spanish Wine Page is to help wine-lovers, both novice and experienced, to find and enjoy Spanish wines. It can also acquaint you with Spain's 50 different wine regions, indigenous grape varieties, labelling laws and lots more besides. This site serves many purposes. It is part directory of facts and figures; part travelogue and guide to Spanish produce; part buying guide with tasting notes and sourcing information. The written English is of a very high standard and the more discursive sections strike an easy and very readable tone.

The site is very well informed with the author's own expertise shining through, plus contributions from experts in particular fields.

This site uses frames to offer a permanent navigation bar down the left hand edge of the screen, which links to all major sections. Note that the links to Rioja Wine Shops and Spanish Wine Shops break this convention and the navigation bar disappears. There's a link back to the main site at the bottom of these pages, but it's a rather messy set-up.

A non-frames version can be found, which works with any browser, at vino.eunet.es/vino/vino_page.html .

SPECIAL FEATURES

Just Tasting/Dirk on Rioja These two sections of the site comprise a huge collection of excellent tasting notes on Spanish wines. Dirk Becker's collection of Rioja notes numbers into the hundreds and extends back to 1995. More general Spanish wine notes under Just Tasting.

References Useful selection of advice and guidance on getting to know the wines of Spain. Included are explanations of Spanish wine terms and labelling regulations, advice on how to build a representative cellar of Spanish wines, guides to the wine regions, maps and more. There are also lots of statistics on wine production and exports.

Winery Visits This section is crammed with information and is essential reading if you are planning a break to Spain's major wine areas. It includes suggested itineraries for visiting Rioja or Ribera del Duero, maps, hotel and restaurant addresses, winery information and more. Even Tenerife wineries are included if you get fed up with the beach!

Wine of the Week Tips on inexpensive wines are added weekly. You'll have to hunt them out in UK shops, however, as suppliers are not listed.

OTHER FEATURES

Madrid Dining The author's rundown on places to eat and drink well in his home town; sample menus and wine lists are provided. The Rioja Wine Shop is an offshoot of the site, selling a good range of wines and shipping anywhere in Europe.

This is a very authoritative site on the wines of Spain which manages to strike a balance between objectivity and the fact that it is so obviously trying to plug the wines, food and culture of the country. The interface is not the slickest in town, but it is very useable and features the kind of specific material unavailable on more general wine websites.

www.wineoftheweek.com
Wine of the Week (New Zealand)

Overall rating: ★★★★			
Classification:	Enthusiasts	Readability:	★★★★
Updating:	weekly	Content:	★★★★
Navigation:	★★★★	Speed:	★★★★

NZ

Wine of the Week is the work of New Zealander Sue Courtney. The title is misleading as in fact this is one of the best resources on the Web for info on the wines, regions and wine people of New Zealand. Sue does indeed have a Wine of the Week, but the site's real strength is as a source of information, tasting notes and articles on all wine things New Zealand. There are a host of absorbing and well written articles from Courtney, who is wine columnist for the local Rodney Times. There are masses of wine and restaurant reviews, dozens of in-depth profiles featuring key figures in the New Zealand wine scene and many fascinating pieces gathered under the headings of Wine News and Wine Stories. This is a site with far more to it than many in terms of interest and readability, and the style is friendly, not too technical and full of obvious enthusiasm.

Courtney does her research and knows her stuff. The opinions expressed are entirely her own, and are therefore subjective, but this is a site that can be relied upon.

The homepage of the site has links to all the most current features clustered around a central image, and a navigation bar at the foot of the page linking to the site's main subsections. It is slightly confusing at first that on visiting any other page the navigation panel jumps to the left hand edge of the screen, but once you realise that it makes for easy navigation as it is applied consistently.

SPECIAL FEATURES

Wine of the Week Each of Courtney's choices comes complete with a photograph of the bottle label, background information and a full and entertaining tasting note. The ratio of New Zealand wines is high, though wines from other areas do feature occasionally. At the foot of the current Wine of the Week is a link to the archives where you will find past title holders going back to November 1998 which makes for a very valuable resource.

Personality of the Week is a slight misnomer as these profiles are actually added less frequently, perhaps once per month. Once again, a link at the bottom of the current profile takes you into the archives. These pieces are fascinating, each one a human story illustrated with photographs. Here are genuinely interesting tales of New Zealand wine folk: makers, merchants and amateur enthusiasts with something to say. You can read interviews with everyone from internationally acclaimed Australian guru James Halliday, to not so internationally acclaimed sales manager Maree Buscke from Gisborne, whose passion for wine earns her a place.

Wine Stories This is a collection of Courtney's wine columns in the Rodney Times. There's the best part of 100 full articles here, on general wine subjects ranging from 'Rosé Wine — a pleasant change for summer quaffing' to 'Vineyard Dreaming — A suggestion of how to start your own.' Once again, a lot of the material is centred on New Zealand, but not exclusively so.

News A regularly updated look at major or just interesting wine news, particularly pertaining to New Zealand. Typical would be a report in the Independent newspaper which listed three Kiwi wines in a Top 50 of the year, or news of the devastating storms that ravaged the Australian crop in February of this year.

OTHER FEATURES

There are local restaurant reviews, a selection of wine links, both to other Wine of the Week sites around the world and to New Zealand resources, and Read of the Week book and magazine recommendations.

With around 70 per cent of New Zealand's wine exports going to the UK, this site will have broad appeal. Though there is an official web site for New Zealand wine at www.nzwine.com which contains maps, links and great information, Courtney deserves attention because of her obvious love and dedication for the wines of her native land. She has also managed to produce a site that combines expertise and approachability very nicely indeed.

---

www.suite101.com/welcome.cfm/california_wine
California Wine

Overall rating: ★ ★ ★			
Classification:	Enthusiasts	Readability:	★ ★ ★ ★
Updating:	Monthly	Content:	★ ★ ★ ★ ★
Navigation:	★ ★ ★ ★	Speed:	★ ★ ★ ★

(US)

The excellent California Wine is housed by a website called Suite 101, which is an online community offering free space for enthusiasts to publish their own sites on a whole host of topics.

Editor Alan Boehmer has amassed an extensive body of articles here. He is a natural communicator and his writing style is casual and discursive, with minimum jargon and the emphasis on clarity and friendliness. That is not to suggest his articles lack depth: not at all. There are strongly held opinions on display and evidence of both great knowledge and enthusiasm.

Boehmer does his research and knows his stuff. Whether he is simply recommending Californian wines to accompany sushi, or taking a philosophical, millennium-inspired look into his crystal ball on the future of the Californian wine industry, he does so with a quiet authority and from a balanced viewpoint.

The buttons in the green panel along the top of the screen link to other parts of Suite 101: they do not form part of California Wine's own navigation. Finding your way around the site itself is quite straightforward. Beside a photograph of rolling Californian vineyards you will see a little panel of four links to the site's sections: Welcome (the homepage); Articles; Links; Discussions. This panel is available on every screen. The Welcome page also has highlights from lots of articles that are most current, but these are also available by going to the individual sections.

SPECIAL FEATURES

Articles Boehmer's prodigious output of quality articles puts many glossier websites to shame. Over 80 full length pieces span topics from 'The Italian Renaissance in California Wine' to 'Wine Touring in Santa Barbara County' to 'Best of Both Worlds', an informal comparative tasting of top red Bordeaux and Californian Cabernet Sauvignon. The pieces are interesting and though-provoking; informative and occasionally enlightening. As noted, the writing style is casual but straightforward: there are few attempts at humour; few polemic rants. Boehmer is quietly professional about his business and he is thorough, doing a splendid job of educating and entertaining.

Links A sizeable selection of Links, with the emphasis on sites dealing with Californian wines or otherwise of Californian interest, though not exclusively so. There are full reviews of each site, and Boehmer's rating from one to five stars for interest. This is a selective and well-chosen set of the best of the Web. Essentially Boehmer offers this page to his visitors as a portal to California information that is missing on his own site. For example he points out www.Wines.com as a site with an extensive list of Californian winery links.

Discussion Forum California Wine's discussion area confines itself pretty much to chat about topics of local interest. It's not a terribly active forum, with weeks passing between posts at times, but the input from Boehmer and his visitors is of good quality and it might be worth checking now and again if you have an interest in the wines of the Sunshine State.

OTHER FEATURES

Clicking on Boehmer's name on the Welcome page displays a nice little pen picture of the man behind the site. You can read about his professional wine involvement and personal wine interests, as well as a general biography of his life and lifestyle. You can even see a photo of Boehmer and his cat, Edwin.

This site doesn't set out to be a comprehensive one-stop resource site on California and its wines. There are no maps, no directories of wineries, no extensive catalogue of tasting notes: Boehmer concentrates on writing about his interests and passions and leaves the keeping of such reference materials to the multitude of other California-based websites out there. His links will point you to those, but this is as good a collection of subject-specific writings as you will find on the Net.

www.winepage.de				
The German Wine Page				
Overall rating: ★★★				
Classification:	Enthusiasts		**Readability:**	★★★
Updating:	Irregularly		**Content:**	★★★★★
Navigation:	★★★		**Speed:**	★★★
G				

Established in 1995, this site is a labour of love for author Peter Rhurberg, a native of Germany who claims he only discovered German wines whilst a student in Edinburgh! It is not the flashiest site on the Web, and it looks quite amateurish in an increasingly sophisticated cyberworld, but it has the best content of several sites devoted to German wines and it is easy to digest. Rhurberg's written English is good and he speaks plainly, but with authority. His essays on topics like Leibfraumilch are blunt and opinionated (it's safe to say he's not a huge fan). He does a decent job of trying to clarify some of Germany's obscure wine laws and regulations.

The reference material in this site is up to date and very reliable. Rhurberg's tasting notes and comments on German vintages, the quality of different regions and grape varieties are also of a very high standard.

The home page has a long list of links to the site's dozen or so sections. At the foot of every section and lower-level page is a link back to the home page. It's not exactly flexible, but it is straightforward enough.

Load speeds are variable: good with the text-only pages or those with simple graphics. A few pages are long and take a little while.

The bulk of the material is pretty static reference data, though tasting notes are added on a more or less monthly basis.

SPECIAL FEATURES

Regions and Producers An active map lets you click on a wine region for a complete run down on the area, its geography and history, grape varieties grown and top producers. The author adds his own comments on the style and quality of wines from the region and provides links to further reading and relevant websites.

Labels One of the greatest barriers to appreciating the best German wines (which are far removed from cheap, off-dry plonk) is understanding their complex and intimidating labels. This guide does a fine job of explaining what each labelling term actually means and gives you the necessary detail to make an informed choice.

Vintages In a marginal vine-growing climate like much of Germany, vintage can be all important. This gives a quality rating to all vintages back to the 1920's, along with a detailed report on vintages in the 1990's. A very useful resource if you are buying German wines.

Tasting notes Rhurberg has amassed a significant collection of well-written notes on wines he has tasted over the years since 1997. The vast majority of these are for German wines. A search facility is badly needed, as the chronological listing isn't too useful if trying to find a note on a particular wine.

Essays Rhurberg gives vent to his frustrations with a small selection of essays. Titles include: 'What's wrong with German wine?' and 'Dry or sweet?', a study of the issues surrounding moves in the German wine industry to re-style their wines according to the marketplace.

OTHER FEATURES

There's a good deal of background information and educational material on buying, ageing and serving German wines, on matching German wine with food and on the finer technical details of must weights and sugar levels. The history of German wine-making is also covered and reference sections offer suggested further reading and links.

The German Wine Page is thoughtful and well researched. Not a glossy commercial site, it presents opinions warts 'n all, but always from the position of someone who clearly loves the subject. There's something here for everyone, from those needing to be tempted into discovering what Germany has to offer beyond Blue Nun and Black Tower, to established enthusiasts who want hard data and considered opinion.

www.cucina.italynet.com/vini
Italian D.O.C. Wines

Overall rating: ★★★			
Classification:	Commerce	Readability:	★★★
Updating:	Irregularly	Content:	★★★★
Navigation:	★★★	Speed:	★★★★

(IT)

There is excellent information on Italian wines, regions and producers on this site, though being Italian the English in the reference sections is a little formal and stilted. Other sections are more approachable, though there is some very odd information under the General heading. How about this from the wine and food feature: 'A sweet-sour preparation, like duck in orange sauce or with cherries, can be matched only by a fortified wine'. That's about as daft as pedantry gets!

It is a very simply organised site with a set of half a dozen links gathered under the General Information heading on the homepage. Each of these takes you to a reference section, which has one single navigational option, a button back to the homepage. Below General Information, you are invited to Choose the options of D.O.C., Region or Type.

SPECIAL FEATURES

Italian Wines by Region D.O.C. stands for Denominazione di Origine Controllata, only one of four levels of classification within the Italian system, but a huge and by far the most important one under which most quality wines on sale are to be found. In this section of the site an active map of Italy is divided into 20 principal wine-producing regions. Click on this for a detailed map of the region and a list of the D.O.Cs to be found there. For example, click on Tuscany and a list of its 22 D.O.Cs is presented. Click on one of these, say

Chianti, and a table of excellent, comprehensive information appears. It includes history, geography, grapes planted and wines made, statistics on production volumes, and a whole host of technical data. A little panel on the right breaks the D.O.C. down into smaller zones if applicable. Below this table is a long list of producers: this is the definitive list, presenting all producers in the region in alphabetical order. For Chianti there are literally hundreds of entries. Click on any of them for full address and contact details.

Wines by D.O.C. and Wines by Type are two alternative ways of querying the same information. The first simply presents all 250 or so D.O.C.s in alphabetical order, letting you scroll down until you find what you want. The second attempts to list the wines alphabetically by Type. This doesn't work quite so well, since Type can be something like Chardonnay (a grape variety), Pasitto (a method of production) or even Rosso (meaning red): a rather long list.

General Information The reference section of the site, not solely concerned with Italian wines. It contains: Wine Producers; Wine Tasting Methods; The Shape of Drinking; Serving Temperature and Combining Food and Wine. Despite the rather pedantic tone, these are decent features, particularly the section on wine tasting techniques.

A particularly comprehensive site within its strictly defined area, Italian D.O.C. Wines is a fine resource. It does not of course deal with some of Italy's most exciting wines currently, such as the Super Vino de Tavola or the newest Indicazione Geografica Tipica (IGT) classification, which is making news in the way that France's Vins de Pays wines have been doing over recent years. For a wider, but not so detailed view of Italian wine and food, try www.gamberorosso.it/e the site of the Gambero Rosso magazine. Meanwhile, Italian D.O.C. Wines is easy to use and a rich source of hard data.

---

http://sol.brunel.ac.uk/~richards/wine/ukvines.htm
Vineyards and Wine-making in England and Wales

Overall rating: ★ ★ ★			
Classification: Enthusiasts		**Readability:**	★ ★ ★
Updating:	Frequently	**Content:**	★ ★ ★ ★ ★
Navigation:	★ ★	**Speed:**	★ ★ ★ ★

UK

It has to be said from the outset that this site is a bit of a hodgepodge in terms of style and layout, with some pretty awful colour schemes and messy formatting. However, if you have an interest in the wines of England and Wales then enthusiast Oliver Richardson's passion and expertise shine through to provide a significant resource. There is a wealth of detailed information about English and Welsh wines that overcomes the amateurish layout. Definitely higher on content than on style.

Richardson clearly knows this subject inside out and has a great deal of first-hand knowledge of the wines, regions and wineries under discussion. There are profiles of at least 100 tourist-orientated vineyards in England and Wales, accompanied by lots of maps and addresses, guides to grapes and wine styles, and useful background information for the potential visitor.

Most pages feature a panel at the top of the screen that is split into two panes. The left-had pane contains a navigation centre with links to the site's eight main sections. The right-hand pane changes according to which of these main sections you are in, and features an index of sub-sections. This is not entirely consistent however, and sometimes the navigation panel is missing, sometimes it is there but looks totally different. There is usually a link to Home somewhere on the page!

SPECIAL FEATURES

Vineyards A rundown on all the vineyard areas of England and Wales including detailed information on producers, soils, climate and wines produced. Richardson gives his own opinions and there are maps, directions and contact numbers for producers.

Wine Making A particularly thorough guide to wine production, including profiles of various pioneers of the English and Welsh scene, history and wine-making techniques. There are also interesting essays on the marketing of English wines and a photographic calendar of the wine-maker's year.

Sources and Stats A detailed and academic reference section giving statistics on production and sales of English and Welsh wines. It also suggests a further reading list and provides links to online resources.

Northern Europe is a rundown on other countries, such as Eire, Scandinavia, Holland and Belgium whose wine production has parallels with the UK. The amount of information on each region varies considerably, according to the extent of commercial winemaking. Typical details include: a history of viniculture, varieties of grapes cultivated in the region, extent and location of vineyards (including contact details if open to the public), and details of associated wineries and where the wine is available to buy.

OTHER FEATURES

Grape Types is not only a grape-by-grape listing of all varieties grown in the region, but a well-informed introduction to the particular challenges of growing vines in a marginal climate like that of the British Isles.

English and Welsh wines are very much under-appreciated at present, few people realising just what level of quality they can achieve (particularly some superb sparkling wines!). Although this site's appearance and functionality is undoubtedly rather amateurish, it is a fine and comprehensive reference for anyone with a general interest in the wines of England and Wales or for those who are planning a visit to the vineyards.

www.frenchwinesandfood.com			
Wines and Food from France			
Overall rating: ★★★			
Classification:	Commerce	**Readability:**	★★★
Updating:	Varies	**Content:**	★★★★
Navigation:	★★★★★	**Speed:**	★★★
(FR)			

In scouring the Web for a French wine site it was difficult to find one in English which offered a balanced overview and covered the country. Though there are good regional sites covering Bordeaux or Burgundy for example, this site, sponsored by the French Ministry of Agriculture, was one of the few that took a national view. Though basically a promotional puff for the produce of France, it is a user-friendly and very nicely executed site that does have a lot of useful information. (A good alternative, but only for those with a smattering of French, is: www.france-vin.com.) The information is presented in brief, bite-sized chunks. This is not the place for in-depth analysis or technical background, but for friendly and approachable introductions to French regions, grapes, wines and food.

Again, the obvious caveat that is on all promotional sites applies, but the factual information and advice look sound, on food and wine matching for example, or on wine-tasting techniques.

The home page features a navigational bar along the top of the screen. This shows colourful cartoon icons for the site's half dozen main sections, and below each a list of links to individual pages within that section. All pages of the site carry this same Navigation bar, so it is easy to move between pages or sections at any point.

Load speeds are average to good, the playful cartoon theme that runs through the site adding a little to the download time.

There is a calendar section that carries up-to-date information on French food and wine events (fairs and festivals around the world), but most of the site contains static reference material.

Some downloadable features (such as a vintage chart) require the widely available Adobe Acrobat Reader. Audio guides to pronunciation require sound capability.

SPECIAL FEATURES

About French Wine This is a collection of resource material. Wine Regions includes a nice interactive map of France that will highlight and name each region as your mouse hovers above it, and will take you to a brief description of the region with further links. Grape Guides are fairly limited, but do include pronunciation advice. Wine Classifications explains France's wine laws. The Vintage Chart requires Adobe Acrobat Reader software.

Entertaining A useful section mostly concerned with matching wine and food and serving wine in optimum condition. Food and Wine Pairing begins 'Rule #1: There are no rules!' which is a good philosophy. It goes on to give useful guidelines and some specific ideas for matching classic French wines to particular foods. Wine Tips offers advice on serving temperatures, glassware and how much wine to allow for dinner parties. There's even a section on Recipes that includes both pre-dinner cocktail ideas and a selection of dishes featuring French cheeses.

Fun Stuff Here are a couple of entertaining ideas: Make Your Own Label let's you do just that: enter some details into an on-screen form and at the click of a button a personalised wine bottle label appears on screen that you can print off and affix to a bottle of your choice. How do you say ... is a pronunciation guide to lots of French wines and wine terms. You can read a phonetic guide, but will need the Real Player software to hear an audio guide (a download button is provided).

OTHER FEATURES

Resources is a section that offers news of French food and wine events and some links to other French web sites.

Fromage is a celebration of France's wonderful cheeses, and Featured Products is a selection of recommended wines, but clearly from producers who have paid to feature.

Rather superficial in terms of depth of content, but a reasonable introduction to the regions and wines of this enormously influential wine-producing country. Some of the links are good too, and it is without doubt a very user-friendly Web site.

OTHER FRENCH REGIONAL SITES OF INTEREST

Alsace
www.alsacewine.com

Bordeaux
www.bordeaux-wines.com

Burgundy
www.bivb.com

Champagne
www.champagnes.com

Loire Valley
www.vins-valdeloire.com

Provence
www.vins.enprovence.com

Rhône Valley
http://www.vins-rhone.com

The Southwest
www.vins-du-sud-ouest.com

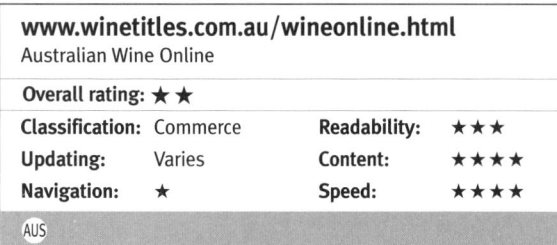

www.winetitles.com.au/wineonline.html			
Australian Wine Online			
Overall rating: ★★			
Classification:	Commerce	Readability:	★★★
Updating:	Varies	Content:	★★★★
Navigation:	★	Speed:	★★★★
AUS			

A site firmly focused on evangelising for Australian wines in general, and its own signed-up wineries specifically, is hardly the place for objective criticism or recommendations. But the Australian Wine Online site is also a rich resource with quality reference materials, excellent articles from top contributors and good links to all things Australian on the Web. The site is made up of reports drawn from many sources so quality is variable, but generally quite high since much of the material is drawn from industry sources and official publications.

The homepage features a navigational panel centre screen with more than a dozen links to feature sections of the site. Within most of these navigational choices appear down the left hand edge of the screen, though not exactly the same set as the homepage. The navigation links are repeated at the bottom of longer pages. On some interior pages the side panel disappears and only top and bottom of page links are available.

Updating varies in different areas of the site. A News section appears to be updated several times per month. The rest of the material is largely static.

SPECIAL FEATURES

Winery Search The site also has a section entitled Wineries but it is only a very limited selection of their paid-up members. This is far more useful: a service that will let you query a database on winery name, brand name, state, even wine-maker first or last name. The result is a very comprehensive little fact sheet with contact information, a list of all brands produced, visitor information, export information and a brief company profile. There is also a link to their website if they have one.

Varieties Varietal reports on grapes: Sauvignon Blanc, Pinot Noir, Merlot, Semillon, Chardonnay and Cabernet Sauvignon. These are drawn from the Australian Wine Industry Journal (as is much of the site's content). The reports are excellent: in-depth, crammed with information and complete with tasting notes for several wines in each category. It's odd that two of Australia's most prominent grapes, the Shiraz and Riesling are not included.

Vintage Reports Very thorough overviews of vintages from 1996 to the present, covering all wine producing regions. There is also a drop-down list of specific regions containing detailed reports filed by wineries in that region.

Regions A very odd section which opens with a clickable map of Australia, yet only four out of literally hundreds of regions are highlighted. The four regions that are covered (Barossa, the Lower Hunter Valley, the Mornington Peninsula and Koppamurra) are dealt with in considerable depth, but this is obviously just a collection of re-printed articles rather thoughtlessly thrown together.

Quiz Everyone loves a bit of trivia, and this ten question quiz on the Australian wine scene will be instantly scored.

OTHER FEATURES

There is a Discussion Forum on Australian wines (though it is not terribly active). A section of Feature Stories has an extremely nice piece on wine pricing in restaurants written by Andrew Corrigan MW, but unfortunately it's the only one! Wine Tours links to a commercial operation organising a wide variety of luxury tours in the wine country.

This curate's egg of a site is by no means the ideal one-stop shop for those seeking comprehensive and impartial Australian wine information. Having said that, the good bits, like the winery searcher or grape reports, are very worthy. As an alternative, Ken Tripp's www.winebase.com.au is the site for his commercial cellar software, but is also a portal to excellent Australian links and wine resources.

OTHER SITES OF INTEREST

The Argentinean Wine Page
www.latinsynergy.org/winery_index.html
Not the most professional of sites, but this largely factual site includes a history of Argentinean wine as well as introductions to the main regions, grapes and wineries. There are also statistics on consumption, production and exports.

Wines from Austria
www.austrian.wine.co.at
Choose the English option on this tri-lingual site for an extremely comprehensive introduction to this high-quality wine country including excellent graphs, charts and technical data as well as fine features on wines, grapes and styles.

Bulgarian Wine Guild
www.bulgarianwine.com
The BWG is a generic body aimed at promoting Bulgarian wines in the UK. This site has everything from detailed maps, to Bulgarian wine and food guides, to a competition to win some wine.

Wines of Canada
www.winesofcanada.com
Very good information about each of Canada's wine producing regions, styles of wine produced and links to Canadian wineries and other Web resources. Also a discussion forum.

Wines of Chile
www.winesofchile.com
The information is rather basic, and only about a group of wineries and their wines, but it does include most of the big names with links to their individual websites.

China Wine
www.gluckman.com/ChinaWine.html
Some pundits have tipped China to one day follow Australia, Chile and Argentina as the next big thing in wine. Much of the country is well suited to vine growing and this small site, basically just a long page by journalist Ron Gluckman, gives the current state of play.

Croatian Wine Page
www.hr/wine
Robert Kostelac is a well respected figure in the world of on-line wine and his information-rich site has maps, introductions, technical data, contact addresses and much more.

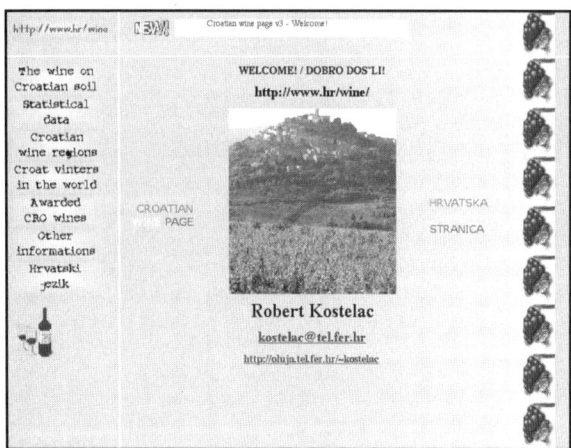

Greek Wine
www.greekwine.gr
This is a commercial site with its own featured wineries, but it is also a very comprehensive and nicely put-together gerneral resource on Greek vines, wines and related information.

The Wine of Tokaji
www.funkcity.demon.co.uk/tokaj2.htm
This site is a celebration of what is undoubtedly Hungary's greatest wine, the sweet Tokaji beloved of Kings and Popes for almost five centuries.

Marsovin Wines
www.marsovin.com.mt/wines
Anyone who has holidayed on Malta might have fond enough memories of the local wines to while away a few moments on this site. Marsovin is the island's major producer and the site includes good introductory information.

Portuguese Wine
www.deOliveira.dk/iwg/w_portug.htm
Marc de Oliveira's basic guide to the wines of Portugal. Home page has a clickable map with tasting notes and data on wine regions. There are also further Port and Portuguese wine links.

Romanian Wines
www.romanianwines.com
Basic information, maps, tasting notes and other titbits on Romanian wines.

The Swiss Wine Page
www.wine.ch
Swiss wine is not so well known outside Switzerland, where they keep most for themselves. The quality is very good though, so this factual, well-constructed site might whet your appetite to go out and find some!

The Zimbabwean Wine Page
www.vicfalls.com/wine
No, I wouldn't have believed it either, but here's the low-down including history, geography, and current vintage news from the delightfully named Monty Friendship.

Chapter 4
wineries

At one time, traditional Old World wineries stayed firmly behind the closed doors of their grand châteaux and let a complex hierarchy of middle men sell their wines. These aristocrats had little need to sell their wares directly, as a reliable band of négociants would snap-up everything they could produce to sell on to eager customers.

But times change and the modern world looks very different, even from the lofty heights of a noble Bordeaux château. Worldwide markets have been carved open through improved transport links and high-tech communications. There has also been the relentless growth and fierce competition offered by New World producers. Now, it is in all wine producers' interests to promote their products directly to their front-line customers. Never before has the serious wine lover had such free and easy access to information on their favourite wines.

The Internet is a wonderful medium for delivering such information. With a half decent website the producer can offer news of the current vintage, a glimpse of latest developments and a potted history of the company to fans anywhere in the world. Predictably, Californian wineries led the way, but this opportunity has been seized upon by winemakers from every corner of the globe. Some have also taken the opportunity to do more than simply showcase their wines, offering their visitors everything from virtual tours and regional recipes, to discussion forums and quizzes.

Australia

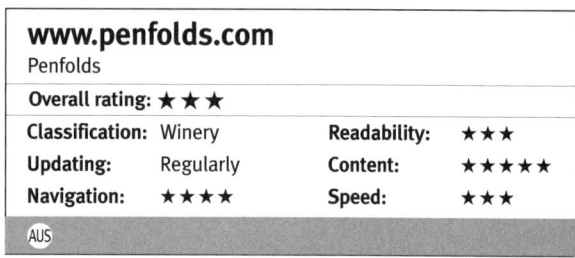

www.penfolds.com
Penfolds

Overall rating: ★★★			
Classification:	Winery	**Readability:**	★★★
Updating:	Regularly	**Content:**	★★★★★
Navigation:	★★★★	**Speed:**	★★★

AUS

Can there be any wine drinker in Britain who is not familiar with the Penfolds name? From their cheap and cheerful supermarket ranges, to the legendary Grange, sold on the international auction scene for thousands of pounds ($24,500 Australian dollars for a bottle of the 1951 recently), this information-packed site presents a wealth of background information to the winery and its wines.

This is the place for definitive explanations and technical breakdown of Penfolds wines. There are also superb overviews of Penfolds principal vineyard sites and their winemaking philosophy and practice.

The bulk of material is on Penfolds products and there is enough technical detail to satisfy even the most anoraky wine-nut. Most of the historical and descriptive information is pitched at a very approachable level. High-quality photographs illustrate and enliven many reports.

Navigation is pretty easy with a navigation bar made up of colourful icons that is always visible in a frame along the bottom of every screen.

The down-loading of pages is reasonably fast. Perhaps the

number of graphics slows this down a little, but it does add substantially to the enjoyment of the site.

SPECIAL FEATURES

The range Every bottle produced by Penfolds is catalogued here, with a full colour image and detailed background to the wine. There is also minute technical detail of the wine and the vintage, along with notes from wine-maker John Duval which make for interesting reading. Specific cellaring and serving suggestions are given for each wine, including food matches. The great thing is that this information is provided for numerous vintages — back to 1990 in most cases: a very useful resource for Penfolds fans.

Winemakers There have only been three chief winemakers at Penfolds in the past 50 years. This section gives biographical details of each, along with a glimpse of the philosophies which have shaped this important producer. The real founding father was the late Max Schubert, the creator of Penfolds Grange. Schubert is arguably the most important and influential figure in the modern Australian wine industry. Single-handedly Schubert lifted Australia's table wine industry out of mediocrity in the 1950s — a time when more than 90 per cent of wine consumed in Australia was fortified wine. This photographic biography makes for fascinating reading.

OTHER FEATURES

Penfolds History tells the story of the company from its founding by a young English doctor who migrated to the distant Australian colony a century and a half ago, to their most recent multi-million dollar investment to turn the Magill Estate winery and associated buildings into an international showpiece.

Events includes details of winery visiting opportunities for those planning a trip down-under.

The Quest for Australia's Best White Wine tells the story of the trials, tribulations and finally triumph of creating Penfolds latest superstar wine, Yattarna.

This is one of the slickest and most attractively designed corporate websites of any winery. It also has a substantial body of highly readable material on both Penfolds and Australian wine in general. A must for fans or for anyone contemplating a trip to Australia taking in a little wine tourism.

OTHER AUSTRALIAN WINERY SITES OF INTEREST

Brown Brothers Wines
www.brown-brothers.com.au

De Bortoli Wines
www.debortoli.com.au

Mildara Blass Wines
www.worldwidewines.com

Rosemount Estates
www.rosemountwines.com

Wynns Coonwarra Estate
www.wynns.com.au

France

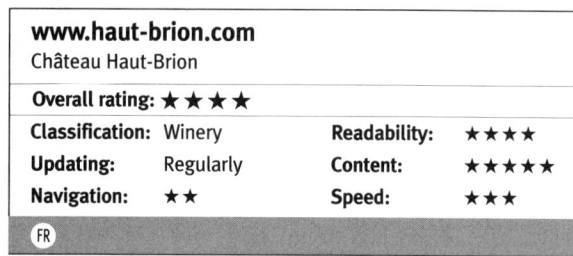

www.haut-brion.com
Château Haut-Brion

Overall rating: ★★★★			
Classification: Winery		**Readability:**	★★★★
Updating: Regularly		**Content:**	★★★★★
Navigation: ★★		**Speed:**	★★★
(FR)			

This multi-lingual site offers much more than a shop window for this venerable Bordeaux Château. For those with a serious passion for the Château, Bordeaux, or wine-making in general, it really is a superb resource. It has the most comprehensive almanac of a year in the vineyard that we have seen on the Web, as well as copious and detailed information on the art and science of wine.

Established in the 16th Century, Haut-Brion is a true aristocrat of the wine world, and as such, their website is a historical treasure-trove of information about the Château and its wines, but it is also a surprisingly lively environment, with a daily news section and active discussion forums. There is a considerable body of high-quality information on this site. It is full of very readable articles, often illustrated with photographs, charts and diagrams.

Navigation is rather inconsistent. The opening screen has a navigation bar at the top of the page, which leads to the main sub-sections. Within these, some screens mimic the navigation bar, others use frames and offer different navigational options. Clicking the Home button sometimes takes you home, but at other times takes you to the Wines sub-section: all rather confusing, though not unworkable.

SPECIAL FEATURES

Wines is one of the navigation buttons on the home page of this site. It offers excellent introductions to each of the Château's eight wines, but Wines is also used to access many of the site's most interesting features which are not linked to the home page by any other route. The opening screen displays a list of the Château's wines. Clicking any of these will present a very detailed and illustrated presentation on that wine: such as grapes used, vinification, and tasting notes.

Along the bottom of the screen (in a separate frame) is a navigation bar to some fascinating sub-sections of Wines. These include:

Seasons A delightful pictorial journey through the year in the life of the vineyard. For example, click on April to see the budding of the vines and formation of new leaves; click on September to see the harvest and sorting of the grapes.

Vintage Detailed reports on the vintage conditions (date of harvest, rainfall and sunshine hours, etc.) for every year from the current vintage all the way back to 1899!

Chais This section is the immensely detailed and educational story of how a wine is made (Chais is French for Cellar). Specifically, it is how the wines of Haut-Brion are made of course, but this beautifully illustrated guide explains every step from receiving the grapes to the bottling line.

Forum Messages to the Forum are welcome in French or English, though the majority are in English. Here fans or scholars of these famous wines can share their passion and ask questions. The Château will happily answer questions such as 'Should I decant my 1983?' or 'How much red wine is made in a year?'

OTHER FEATURES

There is a **News** section which contains latest news about the Château and Bordeaux wines. The site promises that soon there will be a list of worldwide stockists of their wines ; both retail merchants and restaurants. A **Links** page provides a list of good links to wine-related sites.

This grand and prestigious Château has developed a website that is not at all stuffy and offers a lot more for the serious wine enthusiast than a mere shop window for their commercial business. A very useful educational resource that just needs a few tweaks to its navigation.

www.drouhin.com			
Joseph Drouhin			
Overall rating: ★★★			
Classification:	Winery	Readability:	★★★★★
Updating:	Monthly	Content:	★★★★
Navigation:	★★	Speed:	★★★★
(FR)			

Drouhin are one of the best known names in Burgundy. They are both Propriétaires and Négociants, growing and bottling estate wines, as well as vinifying wines from grapes bought from other producers. Widely available in UK shops, the wines of Drouhin span the price range from a few pounds for their basic bottlings, to considerably more for their Grands Crus. They also make wines under the Domaine Drouhin label in Oregon, USA. Theirs is an exemplary web site, with excellent information and plenty of it.

SPECIAL FEATURES

Drouhin Company sounds innocuous, but in fact contains a wealth of information. It contains a complete company history, details of their vineyard holdings, comprehensive introductions to their winemaking philosophy and technical data.

Drouhin Wines is a lovely section of the site. You can Search for your favourite wine, or use the appellation lists to browse their portfolio. For each appellation there is a very nice contour map showing their vineyards, and a list of all wine produced. Click on any one to see a label image, a complete technical rundown on the wine, tasting notes and food-matching suggestions.

Wine and Viticulture deals with viticultural news (including very detailed harvest reports), items on the famous Hospices de Beaune wine auction, and an extremely good section on understanding Burgundy wine labels. There are also good pieces on corks, bottles and glassware.

Vintages covers 1995 to present, with thorough reports on each of their Burgundy appellations and their holdings in Oregon.

OTHER FEATURES

Gathered under the **Generalities** heading there is a small Quiz to see if you have been paying attention, a very good diary of Cultural Events in Burgundy, and even a very nice listing of Michelin-starred restaurants in the Burgundy region that stock Drouhin's wines — and that's all of them!

This is an exemplary website for wine producers. Not only does it have all the background and technical data any oenophile could expect, but it has lots of extras, a simple design and is kept bang up to date.

www.moet.com
Moët & Chandon

Overall rating: ★★★★★			
Classification:	Winery	Readability:	★★★
Updating:	Occasionally	Content:	★★★★
Navigation:	★★★★	Speed:	★★★

(FR)

Moët & Chandon is the one of the world's best known and most popular producers of both Champagne and quality sparkling wines from other regions. This stylish website offers excellent product information as well as more general introductions to Champagne and interesting articles for those wishing to visit the region. Simple navigation is provided by means of a panel on the left hand side of the screen, each section opening in a frame to the right. Watch out for some information panels which pop up as a separate little browser window.

SPECIAL FEATURES

The Champagne Region includes a Virtual Tour of the famous Moët cellars. Explore the 18 miles of cellars, travelling three levels beneath the streets and buildings of Epernay, in text and pictures. Cellars and Visits gives full tourist information. A Dinner in Epernay is a plug for Moët's beautiful Château de Saran, where private guests are entertained. That, unfortunately, is by invitation only, but the site does include a dozen or more mouth-watering haute-cuisine recipes listed in full.

Creating Fine Champagne explains the Moët philosophy and relates vintage conditions for the past few years. The section How Champagne is Made is a nice, succinct introduction to techniques and there is a Glossary of specific Champagne terms.

Our Champagnes offers label images, style guide, tasting notes and food matching suggestions for all the wines in the range.

La Boutique is Moët's partnership with Liquor.com, who will sell you wines from their range as well as accessories, but the $30.00 delivery fee might mean you are better off looking elsewhere.

OTHER FEATURES

Includes a **Champagne FAQ** with entries like 'How much champagne do I need for a party?' and 'What is the best way to chill champagne?' These come complete with answers of course. The section of the site entitled **Moët and Fashion** links to numerous fashion events around the world, sponsored by the company.

A very classy site for an image-conscious product, but there is no shortage of useful information here. Attractive, clean design allied to good content.

OTHER REGIONAL FRENCH WINERY SITES

Bordeaux

Château Cos d'Estournel
www.cosestournel.com

Château Figeac
http://www.chateau-figeac.com/uk/index.html

Château Lafite Rothschild
www.lafite.com

Château Latour
www.chateau-latour.fr

Château Lynch-Bages
www.lynchbages.com

Château Margaux
www.chateau-margaux.com

Château Pichon-Longueville
www.pichonlongueville.com

Vieux Château Certan
www.vieux-chateau-certan.com

Château d'Yquem
www.chateau-yquem.fr

Burgundy

Bouchard Père & Fils
www.bouchardpere.com

Chanson Père & Fils
www.vins-chanson.com

Georges Duboeuf
http://www.duboeuf-beaujolais.com

Domaine Dujac
www.dujac.com

Domaine Jean-Marc Brocard
www.aja.tm.fr/brocard

Domaine Laroche
www.domainelaroche.fr/english

Louis Latour
www.louislatour.com

Domaine Rossignol-Trapet
www.rossignol-trapet.com

Champagne

Champagne Lanson
www.lansonpf.com

Champagne Perrier-Jouët
www.perrier-jouet.com

Champagne Veuve Clicquot
www.veuve-clicquot.fr

Others

Charles Joguet (Loire)
www.charlesjoguet.com

Château de la Tuilerie (Costières de Nîmes)
www.chateautuilerie.com

Dopff 'Au Moulin' (Alsace)
www.dopff-au-moulin.fr

Hugel et Fils (Alsace)
www.vinternet.net/hugel

La Baume (Languedoc)
www.brlhardy.com.au/brands/labaume.html

Chapoutier (Rhône)
www.chapoutier.com

Paul Jaboulet Aîné (Rhône)
www.vinternet.net/Jaboulet

Italy

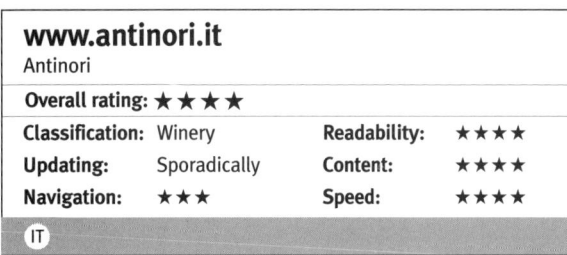

www.antinori.it			
Antinori			
Overall rating: ★★★★			
Classification: Winery		Readability:	★★★★
Updating: Sporadically		Content:	★★★★
Navigation: ★★★		Speed:	★★★★
IT			

The Antinori family has been in the wine business since 1385, remaining family-owned throughout. Today it is directed by Marchese Piero Antinori, a tireless ambassador for his company and Italian wines in general, and also a dynamic moderniser. His Tignanello, the first 'Super Tuscan' led to a revolution in Italy's fine wine industry. The site adds value by including excellent maps, technical information, photo-journals and more. Navigation is easy using the panel in the left-hand frame, though the number of information panels that pop up in separate little windows can be confusing.

SPECIAL FEATURES

Company Profile provides good background information, but hidden away behind text hotspots are some very nice little jewels. Behind the highlighted words Tuscany and Umbria for example, lies a lovely map of the region, with all of Antinori's estates pinpointed. Click on any one for an introduction to the land and the wines.

History reveals the pride Antinori takes in his noble family, traced in this timeline all the way back to 1180.

Mondo Antinori or The World of Antinori, is the colourfully illustrated story of the family, the business, their interests and their homeland. It is nicely told.

Estates catalogues all of Antinori's numerous vineyard holdings through active maps which, when clicked, reveal further levels of detail including varieties planted, areas under vine and tasting notes for wines.

Wines lists all of Antinori's extensive catalogue. Click on any one and a small window pops up showing a selection of vintages, Choose one, and you will see a label image and comprehensive information on the wine.

Recipes come from Antinori's famous restaurant in Florence, the Cantinetta Antinori. This is nicely presented: the four seasons are displayed, click on one, say 'Summer' for example, and a complete summer menu is displayed with full recipe details.

OTHER FEATURES

Includes a clickable map of **Distribution** where you can find the UK agent for Antinori, who will supply you with local stockists. **Related Links** takes you to the Web sites for other wineries in which Antinori has an interest, like the Napa Valley-based Atlas Peak, who also grow Italian varieties.

This site represents a wonderful resource for those interested not just in Antinori, but in the wines and region of Tuscany and Umbria in general. It is packed with good and useful information.

OTHER ITALIAN WINERY SITES

Bava
www.bava.com

Bolla
www.bola.com

Castello Banfi
www.castellobanfi.com

Rocca delle Macie
www.roccamacie.it

Ruffino
www.ruffino.com

Terrabianca
www.terrabianca.com

Lebanon

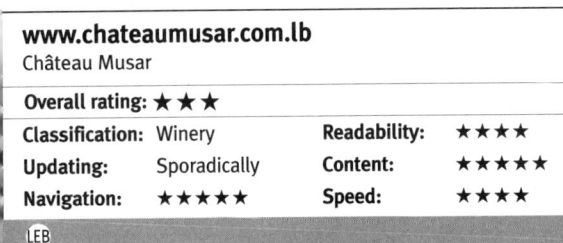

www.chateaumusar.com.lb
Château Musar

Overall rating: ★★★		
Classification:	Winery	
Updating:	Sporadically	
Navigation:	★★★★★	
Readability:	★★★★	
Content:	★★★★★	
Speed:	★★★★	

LEB

Château Musar, sited just 15 miles north of war-torn Beirut, is one of the most remarkable wineries in the world. Merely existing is impressive enough, but that its wines should be extremely fine and regarded by many connoisseurs as equivalent to the best clarets of Bordeaux, is astonishing. The site has lots of information on the Château's history and present-day operation. This is entertaining and illustrated with photographs, and serves as a useful introduction to this amazing story.

It's a smallish site, and navigation is very easy with a permanent navigational panel in a separate frame on the left hand edge of the screen. It links to all the site's sub-sections. There are lots of photographs to be downloaded on almost all pages of the site, but these are small and load times are good.

SPECIAL FEATURES

Profile Here you will learn that the Romans chose Baalbek in the east of Lebanon as the site to build the Temple of Bacchus as their tribute to the god of wine. That sets the ancient historical scene for Musar's current operation, founded in the 1930s, and based in an 18th century castle which can be seen in photographs.

Assets The vineyards of Château Musar are located at an altitude of over 3,000 feet (1,000 metres) in the Bekaa Valley. Vines cover 130 hectares and produce approximately 20,000 cases of Château Musar itself, along with a production of some other wines. You will also learn that the Bekaa Valley, for all its obvious disadvantages, is almost frost and disease-free.

Products This section provides an excellent profile of Musar's wines. For each of the dozen or so wines in its range full vinification details are listed along with tasting notes - in the case of the top Château Musar itself, going back through the vintages to 1959. At time of writing the notes are in French, but translation into English is said to be 'available soon'.

Achievements This section merely hints at the trials and tribulations faced by the gallant winemaker Serge Hochar and his father Gaston before him. They quote Wine Spectator magazines headline that: 'Chateau Musar makes great, ageworthy reds amid the chaos of Lebanon's civil war' when quite literally the Hochars routine work on their vines included clearing unexploded shells and coping with the aftermath of battles raging directly across their vineyards.

OTHER FEATURES

There is a section of press tributes for the Chateau and its wines and contact details for Musar, both in the Lebanon and for its British offices in Middlesex.

This site earns its place in the guide largely on the extraordinary story of the business itself. The website is simple, small and not at all flashy, but the stories it tells are totally fascinating.

United Kingdom

www.hatchmansfield.com
Hatch-Mansfield

Overall rating: ★★★	
Classification: Wine Agent	**Readability:** ★★★★
Updating: Sporadically	**Content:** ★★★★★
Navigation: ★★★	**Speed:** ★★

UK

Hatch Mansfield are an agency who handle the wines of some very prominent producers in the UK. They sell their wines to the trade, acting exclusively for producers in France, Chile, New Zealand and the USA. Their site contains excellent information on the wineries they represent, right down to large tasting notes files that can be downloaded for a multitude of wines. There's also a clickable map of the UK which will list local retailers carrying Hatch Mansfield's lines, but this is not an ecommerce site, so you can't buy. Navigation is via the panel on the left, which is available on all screens.

SPECIAL FEATURES

The Wine List Wineries are listed down the left hand edge of the screen. Hatch Mansfield represents some good names: Champagne Taittinger and Louis Jadot of Burgundy Chile's Errazuriz, Caliterra and Seña, Villa Maria and Esk Valley Estate from New Zealand and from the US, Domaine Carneros and St Francis. Taking Jadot as a typical example of the information provided, clicking their link reveals a thorough profile of the company with photos of the winery and the estate's owners. On the right is a little panel of buttons: Wines contains an overview of Jadot's products, their wine-making philosophy and a list of their wines. Click any one for a label image, more information and the chance to download an Adobe Acrobat file containing extensive tasting notes (you will need an Acrobat reader for this; a download link is provided). Vineyard gives extremely comprehensive details of Jadot's vineyard holdings and their geography. Winery tells the story of winemaking at the estate in pictures and text. Image Files contains scores of very high-quality images of the estate and their wines. Finally, WWW Link will take you straight to Jadot's own website. In all, these producer profiles represent a fantastic resource.

OTHER FEATURES

In Your Store allows you to identify local stockists. The **News** section carries stories concerning the producers within their portfolio. Some of these are very interesting, such as the piece on Errazuriz who are carrying out trials to determine the most favourable way of maximising extraction of flavonoids from red grapes. This follows evidence published by Glasgow University that flavonoids in red wines have very beneficial health properties.

Primarily intended as a support site for the shops, hotels and restaurants who take their wines, Hatch Mansfield have done an admirable job in putting together detailed and well-presented information, probably far more than they needed to. It represents a very useful resource.

United States

www.mondavi.com
Robert Mondavi

Overall rating:	★★★★		
Classification:	Winery	Readability:	★★★
Updating:	Regularly	Content:	★★★★
Navigation:	★★	Speed:	★★★★

US

Mondavi is a giant and very high profile operation whose winery interests are not confined to their Napa Valley home, but have spread to operations or joint ventures in Chile, Italy and all over California. One of the problems with this site is that each of the separate operations have their own web presence, each with its own look and feel. Yet all are gathered under this umbrella site and share some common pages and features. This means there are not one, but a dozen different navigation strategies to understand. Thankfully, there is always a little button back to this homepage somewhere on each individual site. Explore the individual winery sites, but this review concerns itself with the useful features listed in the panel down the left hand edge of the homepage.

There's a lot of good material on this site, from their regular online Newsletter with a dozen features each issue, to an archive of recipes from their cookery school. The site is very professionally put together and the information is comprehensive.

SPECIAL FEATURES

The Online Newsletter is as it says, and very good it is too with a host of full length features not only on happenings on the Mondavi scene, but on wine and food subjects of very general interest. A recent edition featured articles entitled 'The Importance of Terroir', ''The Liberated Enjoyment of Wine with Food' and 'Celebrating 20 Years of Opus One' by Robert Mondavi.

Visiting Our Wineries gives all the details you will need if planning a visit (the tour at Mondavi is one of the most comprehensive on the Napa circuit). Maps are included.

Events and Education has a drop-down list of date and locations where you can see tastings, dinners and demonstrations featuring Mondavi wines. This includes an International section, with UK and other European events.

History gives all the details of the Mondavi family, their winery and wines.

Recipes mostly come from Mondavi's cookery school and form an enormous archive. Many foodies have this site bookmarked just for this section. Literally hundreds of full recipes are listed, along with wine-matching suggestions of course.

OTHER FEATURES

Press Releases A large archive going back to 1997, which makes fascinating reading.

Mondavi's site is pretty business-like and no nonsense. But that means it avoids the flights of hyperbole to which others succumb. The winery information, and of course that recipe archive, make it one of the neatest sites of its type.

OTHER NORTH AMERICAN WINERY SITES

California

Beringer Vineyards
www.beringer.com

Bonterra Vineyards
www.bonterra.com

Cline Cellars
www.clinecellars.com

Far Niente
www.farniente.com

Ferrari-Carano Vineyards
www.ferrari-carano.com

Fetzer Vineyards
www.fetzer.com

Merryvale Vineyards
www.merryvale.com

Niebaum-Coppola
www.niebaum-coppola.com

Ravenswood
www.ravenswood-wine.com

Ridge Vineyards
www.ridgewine.com

Pacific Northwest

Columbia Crest
www.columbia-crest.com

Hogue Cellars
www.hogue-cellars.com

L'Ecole No 41
www.lecole.com

Willamette Valley Vineyards
www.wvv.com

Other Winery Sites Of Interest

Argentina

Flichman Argentina
www.flichman.com.ar

Norton Argentina
www.norton.com.ar

Austria

Lenz Moser
www.lenzmoser.at

Schloss Gobelsburg
www.gobelsburg.at

Bulgaria

Vinprom - Svishtov
www.eunet.bg/eunetweb/vinprom-sv

Canada

Château des Charmes Wines
www.chateaudescharmes.com

Henry of Pelham Family Estate Winery
www.henryofpelham.com

Inniskillin Wines
www.inniskillin.com

Chile

Casa Lapostolle Chile
www.casalapostolle.com

Errazuriz Chile
www.errazuriz.cl

Viña Santa Rita Chile
www.santarita.com

Germany

Dr Loosen
www.drloosen.de

Lingenfelder Estate
www.lingenfelder.com

Weingut Carl von Schubert
www.vonschubert.com

Weingut Gunderloch Nackenheim
www.gunderloch.de

Weingut Kurt Darting
www.vinonet.com/darting.htm

Reichsgraf von Kesselstatt
www.kesselstatt.com

Greece

Winery Skouras
www.skouras.gr

New Zealand

Ata Rangi
www.atarangi.com

Cloudy Bay
www.cloudybay.co.nz

Jackson Estate
www.jacksonestate.co.nz

Neudorf Vineyards
www.neudorf.co.nz

Portugal

Croft Port
www.croft.com

Fonseca Guimaraens
www.fonseca.pt

Quinta de la Rosa
www.quintadelarosa.com

Sandeman
www.sandeman.com

Symington (Dow, Warre, Graham, etc)
www.symington.com

South Africa

Boschendal Wines South Africa
www.boschendal.com

Klein Constantia Estate South Africa
www.kleinconstantia.com

KWV South Africa
www.kwv.co.za

Simonsig South Africa
www.simonsig.co.za

Spain

Faustino
www.bodegasfaustino.es

La Rioja Alta
www.riojalta.com

Martínez Bujanda
www.bujanda.com

Torres
www.torres.es

González Byass
www.gonzalezbyass.es

United Kingdom

Denbies Wine Estate
www.denbiesvineyard.co.uk

Three Choirs
www.three-choirs-vineyards.co.uk

Chapter 5

magazines

The British print media was in stasis through the 1990s as their counterparts in the US embraced the Web as a brave new world of publishing opportunity. Most terrestrial magazines could see the Web only as a threat, while some saw it as more of a joke. The fact that any Tom, Dick or Harriet could publish their own magazine at virtually no expense was a concept they just couldn't, or didn't want to grasp.

In the States things were different. At the most basic level, established wine magazines simply set up shop window sites where the surfer could read a few extracts and fill out an on-line subscription form. At the other end of the spectrum some notable publications poured considerable time and effort into creating Web versions of their magazines that were content-rich. The philosophy was that these virtual magazines not only offered their subscribers added value, but could attract a whole new generation of wired-up wine lovers. Slowly but surely things have been changing and Britain's premier magazine, Decanter, finally bit the bullet and published a substantial website in summer 2000.

This section of the Good Web Guide looks at online versions of the world's wine press, most of which offer regularly updated content. There is also a sampling of the best 'cross-over' sites, produced by wine writers better known for their work in print.

www.thewinenews.com
The Wine News

Overall rating: ★★★★★

Classification:	Magazine	Readability:	★★★★★
Updating:	Bi-monthly	Content:	★★★
Navigation:	★★★★	Speed:	★★★★

US

Yet another US magazine reviewing and rating wines, and yet another website plugging the product by way of excerpts from the current and past issues. Subscribing to the magazine costs a hefty $112 for European readers, but the website, updated every two months, has an extraordinary number of high-quality articles for free. The site itself is simple, easy to use and fairly quick to access. As well as staff writers, The Wine News numbers some big names such as Clive Coates amongst its contributors.

SPECIAL FEATURES

Cover Stories is the major feature from the most recent issue, reprinted in full. These pieces are extensive and well-written articles of genuine interest. For example, 'New Zealand Refines Its Winemaking Niche' is a very considered look at the contemporary wine scene on the islands, including interviews with the movers and shakers and wine recommendations.

Past Issues is slightly hidden away. Scroll down towards the bottom of the home page to find the link. Here is the hidden gem that earns this site its five star rating. What at first appears to be an index of features from back issues, turns out to be an enormous repository of complete articles. All the listed features link to the original article, reprinted in full with photographs. There is a huge range of subjects covered, from 'Smitten by Shiraz' to 'Serving a Champagne

Brunch' to 'The Quintessential Wines of Italy'. There is truly something for every wine lover here. An excellent resource.

Commentary is another full length article from one of the magazine's columnists, usually an opinionated piece on some aspect of the wine industry. For example, 'Raising the Bar on Wine Scores' is a piece by US writer Norm Roby decrying a tendency for wine critics to award too many high scores to average wines.

Feature Story is a full-length feature, perhaps a major tasting event or in-depth examination of some wine-related area.

Cuisine is a feature story on food, with an eye on wine. This is another substantial extract from the magazine, usually including a comprehensive report on some aspect of food or dining, several recipes from in-house and guest chefs, and wine-matching suggestions.

Buyline is the tasting notes section of the website, with an extensive extract from a current issue of those wines that are recommended buys: usually several dozen current releases are reviewed and rated.

OTHER FEATURES

Includes **Complimentary Taste**, an offer of a free trial issue, but unfortunately the offer is limited to US citizens. **Writers** introduces each of Wine News' contributors with a short pen picture.

It would have been easy to dismiss this site as yet another half-hearted and rather cynical exercise in selling. Many such sites tease the visitor with a few paragraphs from the current issue and little more. Here though is an extraordinarily generous and comprehensive collection of serious and professional wine writings, offered freely.

www.winepros.com
Wine Pros

Overall rating: ★★★★★			
Classification:	Homepage	Readability:	★★★★
Updating:	Frequently	Content:	★★★★
Navigation:	★★★★	Speed:	★★★

AUS

James Halliday is Australia's most respected wine writer and has around 40 authoritative text books under his belt. His own site was a Web favourite for many years, but he teamed-up with Len Evans, one of Australia's most prominent wine-makers, to launch this joint venture in early summer 2000. This new site is totally commercial, with ample opportunity to purchase books and wine, but an excellent and sizeable body of wine material has been retained and is free to access. This is largely focused on the Antipodes. Navigation is via a set of natty tabs along the top of the homepage, which present further choices in drop-down menus.

SPECIAL FEATURES

Wine Watch is the first tab in the row, which opens when clicked to reveal a half dozen choices. There are weekly wine picks from Halliday and Evans, Halliday's Top 100 wines of 1999, and a section called Wine Prose that contains a catologue of Halliday's broader writings on wine. The quality is excellent of course, given a writer of Halliday's experience and professionalism. In this section there is a global perspective, with articles on wines, regions and issues from around the world.

Wine Lines includes a substantial body of articles reprinted from Halliday's weekly column in The Australian newspaper. The focus here is relentlessly Antipodean, but the beautifully compiled pieces are very readable. This section of the site also houses Evans@Loggerheads, a collection of musings by Evans on issues affecting the wine world. Pro's Files contains a small selection of articles penned by other writers, most of whom are prominent wine journalists.

Food and Wine is substantially made up of extracts from the now out of print 'Len Evans' Cookbook' along with a few wine reviews from Halliday which happen to recommend a food match. This section of the site lacks substance for now, but it might well improve over time.

Australia contains several full length illustrated pieces, some culled from Halliday's Australian Wine Atlas. These again display a particularly high standard of experise. This section also includes the Regional Spotlight and New Winery Spotlight. These entries will be updated regularly.

World deals with countries other than Australia. There is an ever-changing Country Spotlight which focuses on a specific country in some depth, with profiles of the current state of winemaking and highlights of wines, wineries or people. Around the World is a slightly ramshackle collection. The French entry has a piece on the role of the horse in the vineyards of France and a profile of a single Burgundy estate. Hardly representative of the earth's greatest wine nation!

OTHER FEATURES

You can browse shopping opportunites which pertain to Australia, and sign up for the Wine Pro's monthly email newsletter. There's a calendar of Australian tasting events and a section entitled **Ask the Pros**, where you ask a wine-related question.

A commercial site that, commendably, does try very hard to do more than just sell, sell, sell. The bias towards Australia limits its usefulness, but this is early days for the site and the money and talent behind it promise that it could become a very significant addition to the world of online wine. Worth watching.

www.winespectator.com
Wine Spectator

Overall rating: ★★★★★			
Classification:	Magazine	**Readability:**	★★★★
Updating:	Daily	**Content:**	★★★★★
Navigation:	★★★★★	**Speed:**	★★

US £

The Wine Spectator is probably the world's biggest-selling terrestial wine publication and is hugely influential on the US wine scene. Its Web version has been around for a while and offers a comprehensive and very slick resource for the wine-lover. This is such a huge concern that there's no shortage of information of relevance to an International audience. However, there is also a large amount of information which pertains only to the US wine scene, and so the site misses out on a maximum five stars for readability.

The quality of journalism is high — as would be expected from a major publication — and there is a wealth of authorative material on the site, including a vast repository of archives from the magazine. The fact that it is so obviously commercial and carries so much high-profile advertising might raise questions over impartiality with some visitors.

Down the left hand edge of the screen is a navigation panel with buttons for the site's main sections. A solution had to be found to what could be a very crowded interface in this enormous site, and that has been done rather neatly: as each section button is clicked, it opens up a sub-menu that will stay on screen whilst you remain within that section. It closes-up again when you click elsewhere.

A major drawback is the graphic and gimmick-laden nature of much of the site. This, along with the size of it's databases is presumably the reason that pages can often be slow to download.

The great majority of the site is free to access, but a subscription of $29.95 per annum is charged for access to the full database of over 80,000 tasting notes and to wine auction price files.

SPECIAL FEATURES

Daily Wine News The substantial resources behind the Spectator give it the clout necessary to guarantee access to the latest wine information. This section of the site files dozens of reports each day, from the latest vintage news, to new releases on the wine shelves, to checks on the hottest wines on the auction scene. Though much of the content is of interest primarily to US collectors rather than casual wine drinkers, it is undoubtedly one of the most comprehensive wine newsdesks on the Net.

Wine Search Whether you have access to 15,000 wines, or 85,000 wines depends on you paying your full subscription to the site. Otherwise the functionality is the same: query the Spectator's database by producer, region, wine type, vintage or price and it will show you a detailed tasting note, score and cellaring advice for matching wines. View Others Tasting Notes lets you read what other site visitors have to say about the wine, or you can even pen your own entry.

Library is the central reference point of the site and has hidden depths of wine information. Article Archives lets you read any major article from the print version of the Spectator, from 1994 up to the most recent but one issue. Wine Basics features an ABC of wine tasting, buying strategies, a glossary of wine terms, tips on storing and serving wine and guides to major wine regions.

Dining Another database to query, this one contains 2,000 brief reports on restaurants around the globe noted for their cuisine and wine lists. Don't expect to discover cosy neighbourhood finds: the Spectator concerns itself only with upmarket and expensive establishments. Nevertheless this is a very valuable resource for the foodie tourist with its menus, pricing details, lists of awards and contact details.

Forums The Spectator offers dozens of interactive discussion forums on everything from buying and selling wine, to dining and cooking, to tasting notes. You must sign-in to participate actively, supplying some personal data, though you can browse anonymously ('lurking' in Net jargon). Again, the discussion is heavily biased towards US topics of interest.

Travel Query the Spectators hotel database, or read one of their travel-related articles. There are special 'city issues' which focus on tourism and gastronomy in major world destinations.

OTHER FEATURES

The surface of this mammoth site has only been scratched with the features highlighted above. There are articles galore, competitions, polls and seasonal specials.

Big, glossy and much more corporate than personal, this unashamedly commercial site will possibly divide visitors into love it or hate it camps. It caters mainly for a sector of the American public that views wine very much as a lifestyle product, embracing it along with cigars, European sports cars or stocks and shares: wine as a statement rather than a passion. For all that, it is one of the largest and most professional resources on the web and thus deserves its five-star place in this guide.

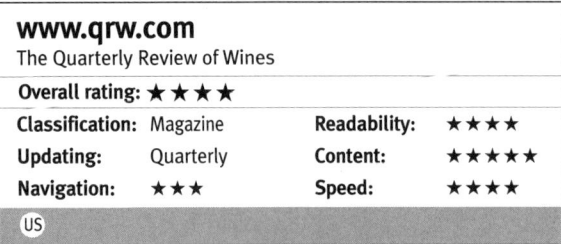

The print version of the Quarterly Review is a glossy magazine with a circulation of over 150 000 in the States, 35 000 of these as in-room magazines for the very upmarket Ritz-Carlton hotel chain. The website is a trailer for the magazine, and contains the full text from perhaps six or seven articles lifted from the current issue. Previous quarters are archived, so in total the site does offer quite a substantial repository of articles, tasting notes and wine news. Many pieces are penned by anonymous staff writers, but the standard of research and their expertise is invariably good. There's also a classy list of contributors that includes top UK wine writers such as Clive Coates, Michael Broadbent and Jancis Robinson.

Down the right hand edge of the home page are the articles from this month's issue. A panel on the left hand side links to general information and to previous issues. This panel is repeated on every page of the site and contains a button marked Main which takes you back to the home page.

SPECIAL FEATURES

Magazine Extracts Between the current and archived issues, the collection of articles collected here forms a sizeable body of material. From useful guides like 'A Shoppers' Guide to California Wine' or 'Wining and Dining in Paris', to reports and special features on the world of wine like Clive Coates' '1997 Red Burgundy: An Uneven Year.'

There are also some nice profile pieces on people and producers like 'A Century of Passion' (from the Winter 99 edition) which introduces the wines and wine-makers of the Napa Valley's Beaulieu Vineyards.

All Things Grape and Small Recently added column, which is a round-up of news and interesting stories from the world of wine. Reports on vintages; corporate news of wine industry takeovers, mergers and bankruptcies; new scientific or medical studies into wine — all this and more are covered in reasonable depth.

OTHER FEATURES

You can of course subscribe to the print magazine from the site ($34.95 for four issues delivered to the UK).

The Quarterly Review is worth bookmarking and checking once a quarter at least for the high quality articles and latest news. It has little to attract you back more frequently, but it's free and simple to use and usually has at least one or two pieces of genuine interest.

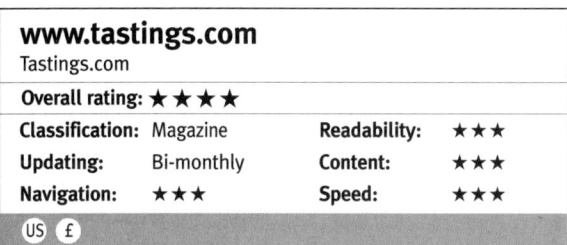

This is the Web presence of the Beverage Testing Institute, based in Chicago, who supply buying guides for wines, beers and spirits which are reprinted in newspapers and magazines. Their own print magazine, Tastings, is issued six times per year and costs $69 for a one year subscription to the UK. This site claims to have reviews of 30 000 wines within its pages. If you want a sneak preview of new reviews before they appear on the web, you are encouraged to sign up for the Insiders' Club which delivers them by email six weeks before they are released to the public. That service costs $45 annually. Navigation of the site is pretty average, with some inconsistency in the way the navigation panel down the left hand edge of the screen is applied. Your first choice is to select from the colourful Wine, Beer and Spirit buttons on the homepage.

SPECIAL FEATURES

Find a Wine takes you to the Winebase, where you can query Tastings.com's database. You may search using Quick Find, or Advanced Find. The former is a simple text box where you can type in any combination of keywords. The latter is a very comprehensive if rather unwieldy form where you can set dozens of criteria such as Score out of 100, Price, Variety, Country and Vintage.

Best Producers List is a list of the top-rated producers year-in and year-out. The idea is that since shoppers often find it difficult to track down the exact vintage of a top-rated wine, this section highlights the most reliable names irrespective of vintage. The long list is sorted by country and grape variety/region. So, for example, you might click on France and then Alsace to see a list of top producers. Strangely, there is no way to go directly to an actual review of these producers' wines from here.

Learn About Wine is a rather haphazard collection. It includes introductions to a few wine regions and grape varieties, technical articles on obscure winemaking techniques like 'Heat Summation' and odds and ends like 'What to drink with turkey'. The pieces themselves are sound, if a little boring to read with no illustrations and a rather dry tone. There is clearly little commitment behind this section, despite their undated claim that 'We will add many more articles in the next few months'.

Wine Dictionary is a nice feature. Enter a word, or part of a word, into the box displayed and the dictionary will find all entries that match. Over 750 definitions are available.

OTHER FEATURES

There is a list of **Wine Stores**, but these are confined to US stores who use Tasting.com's reviews. **Find a Winery** lists over 1500 US wineries with address and Web details if available. **Our Books** is a sales page for books published by the Beverage Testing Institute.

The database of tasting notes and ratings is a very useful tool for any wine lover. The wine reviews are quite comprehensive, and the flexibilty by which the data can be queried makes it easy to home in on specific wines. The interface is a little old fashioned and the navigation could be better, but all in all Tastings.com's vast collection of notes represents a terrific resource for the serious collector or lover of wine.

http://www.clive-coates.co.uk
The Vine

Overall rating: ★★★★			
Classification:	Magazines	Readability:	★★★★
Updating:	Monthly	Content:	★★★★
Navigation:	★★★	Speed:	★★★★

UK £

The Vine is a subscription-only fine wine magazine, published by one of the luminaries of the international wine scene, British writer Clive Coates. The Vine has been published monthly since 1985, and a one-year subscription costs £48.00. This website is a puff for the magazine and Coates' books, but like other similar sites it also contains quite lengthy extracts from current and previous issues that make it worth checking every now and again. It has to be said that the site itself is a bit of a dog's dinner: an unholy clash of colours and fonts, but it works well enough and the quality of content is good.

SPECIAL FEATURES

In this Vine is the puff for the current issue and at first appears to do no more than list the contents of the print magazine. However, a tiny flashing piece of text might just catch your eye: click on the flashing Extract to reveal a lengthy and very useful extract from the current issue. For example, a recent feature was a report entitled '1989 Bordeaux Ten Years On', a superb and highly detailed review of the vintage. It included Coates' observations on how the clarets of 1989 are maturing, plus a comprehensive set of tasting notes on more than 110 of the top wines, complete with cellaring advice. This was followed by a very similar review of the 1989 Burgundy vintage, again with around 80 tasting notes of the leading wines. As a real bonus, a small link at the top of the current extract takes you to Extracts from previous issues where you will find at least one more full length article from a past Vine, usually an in-depth look at a particular fine wine, vintage or region and always including Coates' reliable tasting notes.

Back Issues lists the topics covered in back issues along with availibility and an order form to purchase. However it also features an interesting extract to whet your appetite.

Events is a list of glittering wine tasting opportunities in which Coates is involved. All the details are here if, for example, you fancy joining Coates at a tasting of a 'succession of the finest wines from only the finest winemakers' you will stay in Michelin-starred luxury near Beaune with tastings and dinners in 16th century farm of Becky Wasserman, one of the world's greatest Burgundy aficionados. Cost? A cool $6,350.00 per person. There are slightly less stellar, but just as interesting events closer to home too.

OTHER FEATURES

Other features are very much based around subscribing to the Vine or buying some of Coates' authoritative books.

The hand-knitted feel of the website and its obvious sales orientation could easily make you think there was nothing of intrinsic interest here, but in fact the full-length extracts generously reproduced are of substantial interest to the fine wine lover, and they cover topics of current interest.

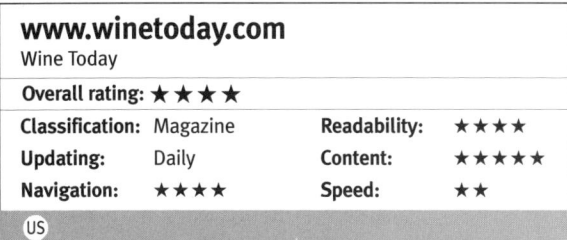

www.winetoday.com
Wine Today

Overall rating: ★ ★ ★ ★			
Classification:	Magazine	**Readability:**	★ ★ ★ ★
Updating:	Daily	**Content:**	★ ★ ★ ★ ★
Navigation:	★ ★ ★ ★	**Speed:**	★ ★

US

Wine Today is a subsidiary of the New York Times. It features reports of consumer and industry news, feature stories on wineries and personalities and has a database of more than 5000 wines. Most of the wines and wineries are Californian, but they claim that 'Our database of wines and wineries from around the world will be increased significantly during 2000.' This is an extremely slick and professional site that is updated more or less daily. Wine Today states that it aims to be 'the wine industry's most timely, authoritative and independent source on all things related to wine' which is quite a target to set yourself. If only it viewed wine from a slightly more global perspective, then maybe the claim would be more credible.

SPECIAL FEATURES

News is one of the most active sections of the site. It features special reports from the wine world, filed every few days by various writers. These reports could cover anything from 'Demand grows for quality kosher wines' to 'Prices cool at Hospices de Beaune auction.' They are of very good quality and usually are illustrated by photographs and links to further reading.

Wine Reviews features Wine Today's assessment of over 5000 wines. There's a Wine Of The Week, a Selection of Current Favorites and a couple of options to personalise this section of the site. First, you can employ the Wine Sleuth to register your interest in certain wines or styles and you will be emailed whenever Wine Today adds a new review that matches your criteria. Next, make use of Personal Wine List to amass reviews in your own folder for printing out as a shopping list at a later date. There is also a powerful search facility. The big limitation is the overwhelming preponderance of US reviews and relative scarcity of wines from other regions.

Wineries is another section carrying a message that Wine Today is in the process of expanding its non-US content. Each winery listing is a detailed snapshot, featuring the people, the history and the wines behind the name, as well as links to the latest news and reviews of their wines from Wine Today. A nice resource, with over 1000 listings.

Opinion is a collection of wine-related articles on topical and contentious issues penned by some prominent US wine commentators: 'Argentina is coming out of its shell' tells the story of the the hidden value of top Argentinean wines, said to rival the world's best; 'Cabernets that won't blow your stock portfolio' bemoans escalating prices for the most fashionable Californian wines, and suggests value-for money-alternatives.

Contests on Wine Today are in the major league with prizes worth thousands of dollars, from digital cameras, to a top-of-the-range wine cabinets. But before you get too excited, the small print (the very small print) states 'Contest is open to legal residents of the United States.'

Community is the site's interactive centre, where you can use the Message Board to 'Share your thoughts and opinions about stories in WineToday.com with fellow readers' or you can sign-up for Abuzz, where members ask wine questions and get the answers from industry experts and other members via email.

OTHER FEATURES

Events A clickable map lets you see a diary of forthcoming wine trade shows and other events in your region. The drawback? The map covers only the States of course, though there is a small selection of events tucked away under 'Events Outside the US' beneath the US map.

A little like its biggest rival, the Wine Spectator (see p.118-119), Wine Today might well be a love it or hate it experience. For the average European its relentless focus on the US is a little irritating, despite their stated intention to broaden their horizons. It is also very commercial, with advertising peppering every page and a hidden agenda of grabbing your demographic details at every opportunity. Having said all that, there is an awful lot of good stuff here, which, together with its professional quality and snazzy interface, might just persuade you to spend some time on this site.

www.wineenthusiast.com
Wine Enthusiast

Overall rating: ★★★★			
Classification:	Magazine	Readability:	★★★★
Updating:	Monthly	Content:	★★★★★
Navigation:	★★★★	Speed:	★★★★

(US)

The slightly confusing home page has links along the top to various commercial enterprises run by Wine Enthusiast Inc. Click on Wine Enthusiast Magazine to see this teaser for the print version of the Enthusiast. Like others of its type it features selected excerpts from the current issue in the hope you will be persuaded to subscribe. However, there is actually a considerable depth of content here, including dozens of Buying Guides, with hundreds of wine recommendations. The site is easy to use and well-written, once again the only drawback for British visitors being a US-centred viewpoint.

SPECIAL FEATURES

Current Issue and Archives contain excerpts from the print magazine. Centre screen are the contents of the current print issue, presented as a table of graphics and short synopses. Only those articles highlighted in blue are reproduced here, and then it is often a sizeable excerpt rather than the whole piece. The homepage also displays a navigation bar down the left hand edge, and one of the links is the Archives. The archive features the previous month's magazine, but this time all major features are included, and you get the full text.

Buying Guide is an extensive selection of wine reviews and recommendations culled from previous issues. This is a rich resource, with literally dozens of themed tastings, each featuring dozens of wines. The Wine Enthusiast tasters give their comments on each, complete with a score out of 100. Many of the wines featured are American, but by no means all. Dollar prices are given.

Vintage Chart is another full-featured section. The chart itself is colourful and easy to use, covering vintages back to 1978 for all the world's major regions and grading each for quality and maturity. There is also a nice report on current vintage conditions around the world. Thoughtfully, Wine Enthusiast provide a button which will send a suitably formatted version of the chart to your printer.

OTHER FEATURES

By and large, Other Features are very much focused on the US. **Wine Links** are mostly to wineries. **Marketplace** has classified ads. **Wine Calendar** highlights forthcoming events. There are numerous opportunities to subscribe to the print magazine, at $39.90 per year for 14 issues.

The Wine Enthusiast offers quite a lot of valuable content on its site and that is invariably of a very professional standard. The Buying Guides are packed with tempting sounding wines, and you could always use the www.wine-searcher.com facility to try to find them in the UK marketplace.

www.weekendwines.com
WeekendWines.com

Overall rating: ★★★★			
Classification:	Newsletter	Readability:	★★
Updating:	Monthly	Content:	★★
Navigation:	★★★★	Speed:	★★★★

UK

Launched in Spring 2000, Weekend Wines is a weekly newsletter which is emailed to subscribers each Friday. It is part of a bank of similar sites published by TalkCast Corporation, on subjects as varied as TV Soaps and the clubbing scene. Weekend Wines contains suggestions for inexpensive wines available from UK high street drinks chains and supermarkets. The website offers you the opportunity to subscribe, as well as a small selection of taster articles and online resources. Registration is required, and the demographic data captured is one of the keys to the thinking behind the site. As part of the registration process you are asked if you object to receiving occasional promotional emails about third party products and services, although you are free to say no, and still participate in the service.

SPECIAL FEATURES
What's in the Cellar? has an archive of previous content from the emagazine. Uncorked features recommended wines, arranged according to who's selling them. The wines fall firmly into the 'everyday' category, running from around £3.00 to £8.00 per bottle. For each there is a brief description and sometimes a suggestion of what to eat with the wine. These are rather simplistic: a Chianti is 'excellent with spaghetti', whilst for a Greek red we are advised 'drink with moussaka', which doesn't exactly fire the imagination.

Vino What's Going On is news from the world of wine. This is a rather odd mix of industry news ('J.D. Weatherspoon's Profits Up') and consumer information ('Drunk in Charge of One Glass', about the dangers of high alcohol New World wines).

A Wine For All Reasons offers a few light-hearted wine suggestions for very specific purposes: if your new boss has invited you over, a Primitivo at £4.99 from Majestic is apparently just the ticket.

How Was It For You? allows visitors to send in their comments on wines they have purchased on Weekend Wine's recommendation.

OTHER FEATURES

There is a small selection of wine links under **More Wine Sites** and to the right of the home page an occasionally updated **Corking Tip**, essentially a little piece of trivia to help you enjoy your wine.

The whole idea of signing up for an emailed service such as this appeals to some, and repels others. The web was once a Pull Technology where Joe Public visited a website and downloaded content only when he wanted to. In this increasingly sophisticated medium there is a move by some sites to swing things in favour of Push Technology so that the site can deliver content whether Joe Public remembers to visit or not. Certainly there is nothing in Weekend Wine that can't be had in any of the Sunday Supplements.

www.foodmad.com
FoodMad.com

Overall rating: ★★			
Classification:	Magazine	Readability:	★★★
Updating:	Weekly	Content:	★★
Navigation:	★★★	Speed:	★★★★

(IRE)

Launched in early summer 2000, FoodMad.com is principally a recipe site, but it covers drinks too. There's a huge selection of cocktail recipes and a decent coverage of wine, complete with articles and recommendations. This Irish site quotes prices in Punts, but many of the stockists given have UK branches too. The site is very uncluttered in design, with navigation options for search, recipes, wines and cocktails along the top of the opening screen. The rest of this review concerns the Wine section only.

SPECIAL FEATURES

Weekly Wine Review and Competition is a misnomer, as on our visits the same review and competition was around for several weeks. More disappointingly, the competition end date came and went and two weeks later there was still no announcement of a winner, or of a new competition to take its place.

Wine reviews are accessed via four colourful wine bottle icons for red, white, sparkling and fine wines. Each features a single review complete with price and stockist, food matching suggestions and sometimes a little bit of background.

Wine Bytes is a short weekly essay on some wine-related topic. This is building into a usefull archive of articles, written in a very approachable style, with titles like What To

Do With Left Over Wine' which offers practical advice, to 'The Hair of the Dog', which features Keane's top 10 tips for avoiding or lessening the effects of a hangover. These are rather lightweight pieces, but they make interesting enough reading.

Whether or not FoodMad.com can keep up its policy of weekly updates will be the key to its usefulness. Certainly the site is attractively designed and the simple concept of a weekly edition offering a handful of reviews, a competition and a short essay could generate a loyal following. They've gotten off to a rather shaky start in terms of update reliability, but it's worth keeping an eye on this site to see how it develops.

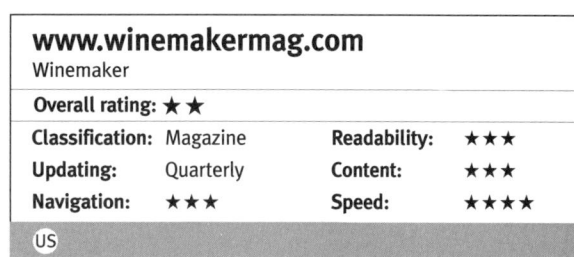

www.winemakermag.com
Winemaker

Overall rating: ★★			
Classification:	Magazine	**Readability:**	★★★
Updating:	Quarterly	**Content:**	★★★
Navigation:	★★★	**Speed:**	★★★★

US

This is the Web site for an American magazine aimed at the home wine-maker. Published quarterly, this is a trailer that features one full article from the current issue, plus a short selection of previous highlights. The articles are detailed and clearly presented, with good technical information that is easy to follow.

SPECIAL FEATURES

Articles Online is a collection of full length pieces from the current and previous issues. Topics are quite varied and interesting within the field of home wine-making, including an excellent article on making flavorful vinegars from left

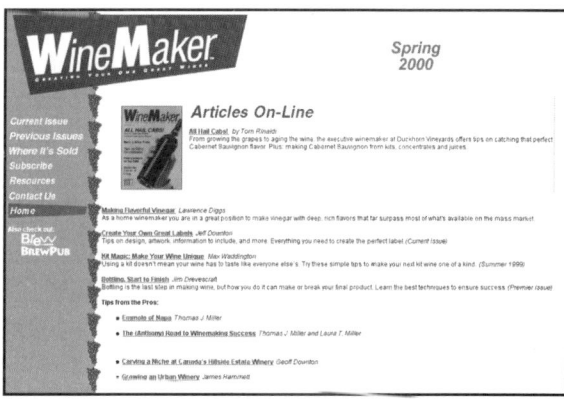

over wine, one on creating the perfect wine label and an interesting guide to tweaking wine kits to transform them into quality and unique wines.

Tips from the Pros can be found by scrolling towards the bottom of the homepage. It contains several interviews with professional small-scale winemakers who are happy to share their experiences and advice.

Resources contains details and addresses for home wine-making clubs, courses and competitions, but these are all confined to the States. However, there are also lists of books and websites that are of international interest. There is also a good deal of technical information within this section, like a table of wine yeasts for example.

The articles and links probably make this site worth a visit for the home wine-maker. The fact that many of the pieces presume the reader has access to some nice, fresh Cabernet or Chardonnay grapes limits the usefulness of some of the advice, but others deal with wine-making from concentrates or other fruits.

www.wine-advocate.com/uk
The Wine Advocate

Overall rating: ★			
Classification:	Homepage	Readability:	★★★★
Updating:	Monthly	Content:	★★★★★
Navigation:	★★★★★	Speed:	★★★★

(FR)

Why is there a one-star website in this book? Well, the question isn't so much why, as who? The Wine Advocate is Robert Parker, the world's most influential wine critic. On Parker's word are fortunes won and lost in the wine business. The print version of the Wine Advocate is a subscription-only bi-monthly journal that reviews and rates the world's wines. Points are awarded to every wine, and a worldwide scramble ensues to snap up the high scorers; whilst the losers are destined to gather dust on retailer's shelves. Unfortunately, this site is little more than a puff for Parker, but its inclusion here is merited because, of the little content it does boast, a page of monthly wine selections are offered as a taster of Parker's latest tips. These recommendations are not otherwise available without shelling out big bucks to subscribe to the print edition ($85 for six issues delivered to the UK). The wine reviews paint a good descriptive picture of what's in the bottle. Parker is not given to verbose flights of fancy when describing wines, but neither are his notes in any way dull.

Parker's influence and his longevity in the business are testimony that he knows his stuff. As with all wine critics, tastes are obviously very subjective and personal, but Mr Parker's legion of loyal fans seem happy with their guru.

SPECIAL FEATURES

Selections of the month Each month a small selection of wines is recommended. The site provides the full text of Parker's review, including his famous points score and guidance on when the wine should be drunk. The site tends to concentrate on newly released wines, and offers a range from everyday bottles, to fine and rare wines: those 95 plus pointers that get the wine world in such a tizz. No stockists or prices are given, which would have been useful icing on the cake.

OTHER FEATURES

Absolutely everything else on the site is direct hard-sell for Parker's magazine or books, or else is a page of starry-eyed reviews of Parker himself.

Well worth a few moments of your surf time once a month to read and print the latest hot tips.

OTHER SITES OF INTEREST

Decanter
www.decanter.com
Decanter is the UK's most influential wine magazine. They have flirted with a token site for years and promise a more extensive version in the summer of 2000.

On Wine
www.onwine.cc
Florida-based Sheila and Ben Bodenstein's wine reviews and articles.

Oz Clarke
www.ozclarke.com
Promotional site for Oz's books, but does have excerpts and links.

Smart Wine
www.smartwine.com
US online magazine concentrating on US wines.

Wine Press Northwest
www.winepressnw.com
Focuses on Washington, Oregon, Idaho and British Columbia's winemakers and their wines.

Wine State
www.winestate.com.au
Fine Australian magazine with tasting notes, forums, recipes and links.

WineX
www.winexwired.com
Wine for the clubbing generation. The Web site is certainly different. Worth checking out.

Wine Brats
www.winebrats.org
Another US site with attitude. Their mission: is to to fight the cultural barriers that have been built up around wine.

Chapter 6
wine accessories

There is a mystique surrounding wine that distinguishes it from any other beverage. The intricacies of how to pass the port at a formal dinner; of whether the 1988 or 1989 vintage was best in Bordeaux; of when to decant a ten year old claret fill magazine pages, newspaper columns and of course, cyberspace.

The average wine lover is also a fanatical stickler for detail.

Show me a wine lover, and I'll show you someone who, to some extent at least, is just as enthralled by the facts, figures and paraphernalia of wine as they are by the stuff in the bottle: collecting the rarest labels, choosing just the right glassware, buying all the latest books.

This section of the Good Web Guide is just for them. It features wine sites that will pander to their weaknesses:

that will sell them the perfect glass for every varietal; will find a copy of the most obscure wine tome and will celebrate the joys of corkscrew-collecting or wine-label swapping.

Within these pages are sites that offer genuinely useful and often quite fascinating services, as well as sites that will simply let you marvel at the spectacular range and depth of obsession displayed by the world's wine lovers.

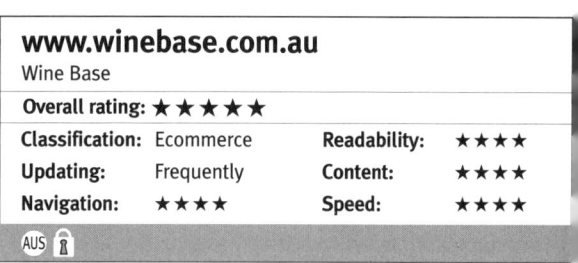

www.winebase.com.au			
Wine Base			
Overall rating: ★★★★			
Classification:	Ecommerce	Readability:	★★★★
Updating:	Frequently	Content:	★★★★
Navigation:	★★★★	Speed:	★★★★
AUS			

This low-key site starts with a friendly 'g'day' on the introductory page. Information about the product — cellar-management software — is presented in a jargon-free, practical manner and there's plenty of it. The site includes many well-written articles on wine by members of the Australian Society of Wine Education as well as a host of other entertaining material.

Navigation is intuitive and simple, with buttons for each of the site's sub-sections in a panel on the left-hand side of every screen. Unfortunately, longer pages don't offer navigational links at the bottom, so you have scroll back up the page to visit another area of their site.

Load speeds are generally very good. The site steers clear of fancy animations and gimmicks, so even those pages with larger graphics (maps and software screenshots) load efficiently, and speedily.

WHAT'S ON OFFER

Products This colourful and user-friendly site is the labour-of-love turned business of Ken Tripp, a wine lover and computer programmer. The software places great emphasis on ease of use. WineBase keeps track of the maturity of every wine in your cellar, finds those that are best to drink now, lets you plan your cellar purchases and keeps track of what you buy and use. It can produce graphs and tables and features easy to use Dialog Boxes that require you to do minimal typing. It comes pre-loaded with 13,000 Australian, New Zealand and US wine-tasting notes, maps and address details for thousands of wineries world-wide. It also has a Web Publishing feature, which allows you to create your own website about your wine collection. WineBase will run on 386SX PC with 2mb of memory and 10mb of free Hard Disk space, but the author states it is happier on a 486 DX or better. A demo version is available for free download.

The Service Orders are processed and dispatched within 24 hours. Product support is unlimited and free (by email, fax or phone).

Product Information There's a raft of information as well as a free demo copy available on the site. Excellent and comprehensive data with screenshots and plenty of comparative charts against competitor's products.

The Ordering Process Very straightforward, one simple form to complete.

More than the Hard Sell? The Wine Base Gazetteer adds hugely to the appeal of the site, being a gateway to a mass of wine information and links, especially about Australian wines. The Gazetteer points to a very substantial collection of resources and this site is well worth a visit for that, even if the product is not of interest. There are articles, maps, links and even a chance to check live reports on the weather in the Australian wine regions.

www.winetours.co.uk
Arblaster & Clarke Wine Tours

Overall rating: ★★★★			
Classification:	Tour Operator	**Readability:**	★★★★
Updating:	Sporadically	**Content:**	★★★★
Navigation:	★★★★	**Speed:**	★★★

UK

Though basically an online version of any tour operators brochure, it is fair to say that Arblaster & Clarke probably give much more detail than most. Within the mini-essays which describe each tour you will find a detailed itinerary. Most important of all for the dedicated wine-nut, a tasting plan of all the wineries to be visited is provided. Navigation is in a separate frame down the left hand edge of the screen. Buttons link to the different tour collections on offer as well as to useful maps and background information.

SPECIAL FEATURES

Tours are the business of Arblaster & Clarke; wine tours specifically. Founded in 1986 by husband and wife team Tim Clarke and Lynette Arblaster, the firm has grown steadily, is fully licensed and bonded, and had substantial experience in this field. They offer everything from Champagne weekends, to Wine Cruises and Cookery Schools. Their Web site does not allow full ecommerce booking of tours, but does have a wealth of useful information. The tour guides used by Arblaster & Clarke's fall squarely into the Expert category. They include several famous names from the wine writing world and several Masters of Wine. The tours themselves are categorised into collections.

Champagne Tours are generally short breaks by coach and Eurostar or ferry. An example might be three days spent in Reims, with daytime visits to a famous cellar such as the ancient caves of Taittinger, and, in the evening, a comparative tasting over dinner. Prices range from around £240 - £280 depending on dates.

Classic Tours make use of scheduled airlines and get you into the tasting mood as soon as possible, usually accompanying lunch or dinner on arrival. Hotels are four star and are generally in a town or village so you can stroll and explore when you wish to. A typical day might begin with a buffet breakfast followed by a wine visit and comprehensive tasting. The second visit might include a leisurely gastronomic lunch of local specialties, accompanied by wines of the estate. What is left of the afternoon would be free, then the tour meets up again early evening for a comparative tasting hosted by the wine guide before dinner.

Reserve Collection is described by Arblaster & Clarke as 'the ultimate wine tour'. Tastings include top growth expensive wines and party sizes tend be smaller. Prestigious châteaux are visited, and deluxe hotels are used — or even the wine châteaux themselves.

Walking Tours are for some the perfect holiday: the chance to combine walking in the rural countryside with winery visits and tastings might have great appeal. Arblaster & Clarke use small family-run hotels with en-suite bathrooms for these tours and the party is limited to 16. A coach is around throughout the tour to move bags, collect wine and shuttle participants to local towns. A comforting thought is that the coach can also be called for you if you want to bale out at any stage!

Other Tours include cookery tours, long-haul tours, wine cruises and coach tours. Arblaster & Clarke are the appointed agents for tours organised by both the Sunday Times Wine Club and the Vinopolis Wine Exhibition on London's South Bank, and a number of events are organised each year for members of both.

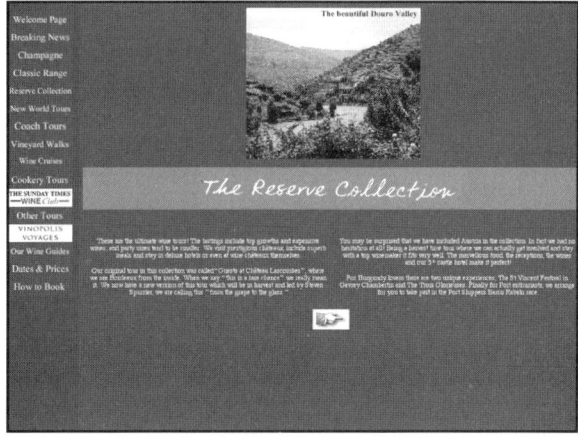

This is an extremely comprehensive website in terms of the information on offer. It lets itself down a little by not having potentially useful facilities like the ability to view up-to-date tour availability or pay deposits online, but that doesn't stop it being a useful resource. Browsing around this site for a while certainly whets the appetite both for sunny foreign climes, and for a glass of something decent.

www.cephas.co.uk
The Cephas Picture Library

Overall rating: ★★★★			
Classification:	Photography	**Readability:**	★★★★
Updating:	Weekly	**Content:**	★★★★
Navigation:	★★★	**Speed:**	★★

UK

Photographers on the Web have a real dichotomy to contend with: photo-quality images take up massive bandwidth and therefore take an age to download, so most are compressed, which degrades the image; but the whole point of their site is to demonstrate the fine quality of their work. The solution found by Cephas is to compromise somewhere in the middle with reasonable quality, and acceptable speeds, though this site is pretty slow at standard modem rates.

The text content here is minimal, which is only to be expected of a site promoting the photographs of the Cephas Picture Library. Where it occurs, it consists of information about the business, copyright warnings and a gentle sales pitch. The photos do carry short captions.

On the home page are a half dozen or so colourful oval Icons which are links to the site's main photo collections. Each photo collection has its own introduction and index page. Wine, for example has geographical categories for the photos, as well as links to other sections such as Grapes and Bottles and Glasses. There is also a button for Home. Within any one of the Categories pages there are buttons for Back and Home.

SPECIAL FEATURES

Wine & Vineyard Photos Cephas is basically the work of photographer Mick Rock. Next time you browse through Decanter or Wine magazine you will be astounded by the proportion of photos that are drawn from Cephas' bank of 100,000 wine images. That vast collection is represented by hundreds of sample images in this site. The Wine & Vineyard Photos index page has collections of French, European, United States and Southern Hemisphere images. Within each you will find a page of small thumbnails. Clicking on the thumbnail will reveal a large-scale version along with a short caption. The photographs themselves are of the highest quality and it is quite fascinating to browse through the collection for a while. Cephas' terms and conditions state that you may make use of these images free of charge, but only in certain strictly defined circumstances. Otherwise, fees must be paid. There are also collections under this heading of photographs of Grapes, Glassware and from Recent Trips.

Other Photos As well as wine and vineyards, there are collections for Food and Drink, Spirits and Beers and Travel.

Exclusive Prints If you fancy owning a high quality hand-printed original you may choose any image from the Web site, or from any book or magazine in which Cephas' work has appeared (and those are many!). Two sizes are available: 12x10" and 20x16" costing £75 and £165 per print respectively, including postage and packing.

OTHER FEATURES

A **News** section tells you about the latest commissions and awards for the company.

A pretty basic site, but one that's of interest to both wine-lovers and photographers I'd imagine; or wine-loving photographers I'm certain! The images are very beautiful and informative. It is slightly frustrating to sit out the 20 seconds it can take for a larger image to appear, but then any further compromise on quality in the chase for speed would have made the whole exercise pointless.

www.winebooks.co.uk			
John Roberts Wine Books			
Overall rating: ★★★★			
Classification:	Bookseller	Readability:	★★★
Updating:	Weekly	Content:	★★★★
Navigation:	★★	Speed:	★★★★
UK			

John Roberts has been a specialist seller of wine books on the Web for several years and his expertise shines through on this site. His very personalised service has become the focus for wine lovers around the world looking for rare and out of print books. This site is little more than a long list of available titles, divided into a main catalogue, plus various sub-categories for specific wine-related subjects. Within each section, books are presented alphabetically by author's surname. Most book listings are accompanied by Roberts' pertinent comments and notes on the condition.

SPECIAL FEATURES

Catalogue of Out-of-Print and Scarce Wine Books lists hundreds of books, divided into a dozen or more categories such as '20th Century Wine Books', 'Wines of France' and 'Sherry and the Wines of Spain.' Within each category, books are listed alphabetically. Almost all books come with Roberts' comment on the book, plus some pertinent points about it. The condition of these old books is minutely detailed, and indeed Terms and Conditions at the foot of the home page explains exactly what to expect from a description such as '89pp, orig. thin card covers slightly creased at one corner, inscribed & signed.' The jackets of several books are also illustrated within the list.

New Books is a constantly updated Stop Press of new stock.

Wine-related bookplates is a collection of beautiful plates from historic and rare wine books - not for sale, but lovely to look at.

Links features a useful set of links to other wine sites. Most of these carry a brief comment from Roberts' and seem to be well-chosen.

There is very much a hand-knitted feel to this site that's about as low-tech as websites come. That however, is part of its charm: Roberts' own passion for wine books is evident throughout and the content is far more important than the style of delivery. An excellent resource for the bibulous imbiber.

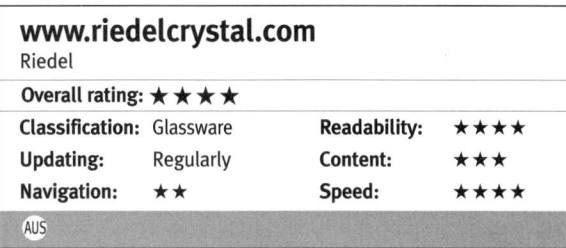

www.riedelcrystal.com
Riedel

Overall rating:	★★★★		
Classification:	Glassware	Readability:	★★★★
Updating:	Regularly	Content:	★★★
Navigation:	★★	Speed:	★★★★

AUS

This Austrian site is information-rich, not only on Riedel's crystal glassware, but on wine-tasting in general and the science behind our perceptions and the evaluation of wine. These are clearly presented and included are learned papers by Yale University professors and entertaining pieces by writers from the New York Times.

The homepage is nothing more than a list of links to the site's sub-sections. Within these there are navigation links at the bottom of each page. On some pages this is a block of colorful icons to most other sub-sections, but on others there is only a link back to the homepage. Beware: the link back to the homepage is labelled Top, which is rather confusing if you expect it to take you to the top of the current page.

WHAT'S ON OFFER

Products Riedel's range of wine glasses has taken on almost mythical status amongst wine connoisseurs. This site provides a mass of background information on the firm's products as well as detailed scientific background on how our senses of smell, taste and touch play a role in wine appreciation. This company manufactures a bewildering range of wine glasses. Basically there are four different collections from the everyday 'Overture' range of machine-made crystal which runs to a half-dozen glasses, to the hand-blown and delicate 'Sommelier' collection which has around three dozen different glass shapes, each scientifically designed to enhance the wine-drinking experience. There is also a collection of decanters. This is not an ecommerce site as such as there are no direct sales, just company and product information.

Product information Making up your mind which of the hundreds of wine glasses to buy is made easy thanks to extensive data on the glasses including construction, dimensions and which wines they are best suited to. There's also a handy 'glass-finder' section which will present all suitable glasses for the particular grape variety or wine style of your choice. A useful section lets you search for local stockists by clicking an interactive map, and there is very good support information on the cleaning and care of these fragile and expensive items.

More than the hard sell? There's a useful collection of wine links, and many of the information sections, such as how to choose a wine glass, and how to care for delicate crystal apply equally to all stemware, not just Riedel's own products.

www.bullworks.net/virtual.htm
The Virtual Corkscrew Museum

Overall rating: ★ ★ ★ ★			
Classification:	Enthusiasts	Readability:	★ ★ ★ ★
Updating:	Frequently	Content:	★ ★ ★ ★
Navigation:	★ ★	Speed:	★ ★

US

Donald A. Bull is, quite frankly, loopy about corkscrews. This site is part museum, part shrine, part swap-shop, and part commercial store selling corkscrews (naturally) as well as books, photos and general corkscrew memorabilia. For those who share Bull''s passion for quirky, valuable and antique corkscrews, this site is a must. For the rest of us, it still makes for a diverting few minutes of surfing time.

Bull lays his corkscrew-loving life on the page and invites you to have a browse. You can read articles on his trip to Atlantic City for the Collectibles Convention, how he learned to fly a glider through a corkscrew-related friendship, or even the dreadful trials of the journey to buy a corkscrew from Joan, who had answered his small-ad in the local newspaper.

Basic is the word that springs to mind when considering the strategy used for moving around this site. The opening screen has a dozen or so colourful buttons, each of which links to a distinct part of the site. The look and feel of each part is quite different: some use frames; some have a table of menu options, but thankfully the one thing you can rely on is a link back to The Virtual Corkscrew Museum (in other words Home) at the bottom of each page.

Bull glitzes-up his site with plenty of colourful backgrounds, high-quality photographs and cartoon graphics. As a virtual museum lots of detailed photographs are to be expected, though these inevitably slow things down. But the download times can be lived with and in truth, many of the photographs are extremely good and detailed.

SPECIAL FEATURES

Corkscrew The vast corkscrew collection is catalogued and categorised by type such as Bulldogs, Cherubs and Golfing. Within each are photographs and descriptions, with often some background information on that particular genre of corkscrew.

Postcard Gallery An even larger collection of corkscrew-related postcards. Bull's collection is presented in categories once again, several of which contain dozens of high-quality images of the postcards. Most of these are antique, and many of them are humorous.

Information Booth Everything you ever wanted to know about corkscrews, and possibly a little bit more. Learn about corkscrews and collecting; read the Corkscrew Questions and Answers section; discover the truth about corkscrews in

Let's go find a really big bottle of wine!

the movies. You can even find out about the role of the corkscrew in Malaysia or Botswana.

Story Room Here is where you can read the accounts of Bull's adventures in corkscrew-land. These articles are lavishly illustrated with photographs not only of corkscrews, but Bull, his car, his dog, his friends - in fact, of anything that seems to take his fancy. Highly entertaining.

OTHER FEATURES

How to Collect Corkscrews is a step-by-step guide for those inspired by Bull's enthusiasm or already intrigued by this hobby. The Club Room has lots of links and information for other collectors around the world. Slide Show is a self-paced leaf through photographs and descriptions of some unusual and valuable corkscrews, and Movie Theatre has lots of movie clips of corkscrews (not corkscrews in the movies, but Bull demonstrating various corkscrew mechanisms).

We have only scratched the surface of this truly information-rich site. Bull's obsession is clearly matched by his knowledge and passion, and there is a lot to enjoy about this up-beat site. Absolutely worth a visit!

www.winetech.com
Wine Technologies — Robert Parker's Wine Software

Overall rating: ★★★★			
Classification:	Software	**Readability:**	★★★★
Updating:	Sporadically	**Content:**	★★★
Navigation:	★★★	**Speed:**	★★★★

US

Wine Technologies is an exemplary site for wine-lovers who need to investigate wine cellar database software, and there's a large amount of background information provided on their products to help you make your purchase. It's easy to browse through their introductory texts and useful screen-shots, which give a reliable impression of what's on offer.

Though a little inconsistent, the navigation is clean, easy to understand and comprehensive. The home page has a block of links in the centre of the screen which access all the site's main sections. On lower-level pages this navigation block jumps to the left-hand side of the screen. Thoughtfully, longer sections repeat the links at the bottom of the page.

WHAT'S ON OFFER

Products There are several pieces of computer software on the market that help you manage the precious contents of your wine cellar. This has the unique advantage of including the tasting notes from American wine guru Robert Parker as part of the package. The site's main product comes on CD-ROM in Standard and Deluxe editions. As well as the all important cellar management database software, the former has 8000 tasting notes from Parker, and the latter has 28 000 along with historical price records for these wines. The software itself helps you plan and track the contents of your cellar and the development of your wines. There's a fast search for wines based on key words which need not be fully typed, Robert Parker's tasting notes automatically link to your wines and you search and sort your wine collection in seconds, seeing the results in colourful reports. Of interest to the wine investor is the Wine Price File, a 600-page book showing market prices for 100,000 wines from 1998 all the way back to 1653. The software requires a 486 or Pentium PC with at least 8MB of memory and 50MB of free hard disk space (75MB for the Deluxe Edition). A demo version is available for free download.

The Service Standard delivery to Europe within 15 working days, and costs $11 to the UK. Priority shipping takes 5 days and costs an extra $15. Special gift-wrapping is offered at $12. Support is provided via email, fax and voicemail.

Product Information Excellent and comprehensive information.

The Ordering Process Pretty straightforward. You choose which products, how many of them, and delivery preferences. Handy drop-down lists save some typing.

More than the Hard Sell? Virtual Cellar Visits is a nice feature: photographic tours of some wonderful personal cellars around the globe. Robert Parker's Vintage Chart is a colour-coded and comprehensive reference to the quality of vintages world-wide.

www.artofwine.co.uk
The Art of Wine

Overall rating: ★ ★ ★			
Classification:	Ecommerce	Readability:	★ ★
Updating:	Infrequently	Content:	★ ★ ★
Navigation:	★ ★ ★ ★	Speed:	★ ★ ★
UK			

There is very little to this site other than product information about the wine storage solutions on offer. That is clear enough, with sufficient comment along with photos and illustrations to be useful.

A navigation bar appears in a separate frame along the top of the screen. This, with its buttons for each of the Art of Wine's product ranges, stays permanently visible making movement around the site quite straightforward.

WHAT'S ON OFFER

Products The Art of Wine's specialty is all aspects of wine storage equipment for the home or other situations where there is no traditional cellar. Their North London showroom displays the range of solutions that are available, but for the ambitious wine collector outside the Capital this easy-to-use Web site gives all the detail. This is not an ecommerce site, so online ordering is not an option.

Art of Wine are both designers and builders of customised wine cellars, and re-sellers of wine storage equipment. Basically their solutions fall into three categories: temperature and humidity-controlled wine storage cabinets which allow for the storage of wine in optimum conditions regardless of the ambient temperature (from 50 to 200 bottle capacity); cellar air-conditioners that will convert any space into a cellar; conventional racking systems, from conventional pigeon-hole racks to luxury racking solutions from America and France. Art of Wine also offer a cellar design service, where they will design the layout of the optimum cellar using Computer-Aided Design software. This can be done by post, based on a floorplan supplied by you.

Product Information This is pretty good, with detailed photographs of all products as well as descriptions and tables of dimensions or capacity, as well as full technical specification for the electrical storage devices.

More than the Hard Sell? Not much to be honest. Browsing through the catalogue does raise the issues surrounding the storage of fine wines, and you can spend a few minutes daydreaming of what you'd do if you had the space and money for one of the fabulous cellars illustrated.

www.winetag.com
Wine Glass Name Tags

Overall rating: ★ ★ ★			
Classification:	Wine Tags	**Readability:**	★ ★ ★
Updating:	Sporadically	**Content:**	★ ★ ★ ★
Navigation:	★ ★ ★ ★	**Speed:**	★ ★ ★ ★

(US)

This company offers a unique product that might just appeal to those throwing a wine party, or involved in the wine business. Based in the USA, but shipping worldwide, the company manufactures individual tags which fit round the stem of a wine glass: little foil discs that come pre-printed or can be custom designed. Their comprehensive site offers all the information you need to choose and order and navigation is easy using a panel on the left hand side of the screen. This is not a full ecommerce site, so although you can add and remove things from a shopping basket and send off and order form, the sale transaction is completed by telephone. International shipping is at cost.

SPECIAL FEATURES

Wine Glass Name Tags is the company's standard range. This is divided into a number of categories, from blank tags which you can write on, to designs for wine tastings, birthday parties, weddings and any other occasion you can think of, from 'Merry Christmas' to 'Happy Hanukkah.' Every design is illustrated and described, and beside the price are boxes for Quantity and Add to Basket so you can shop as you browse. Prices run from $3.99 to $4.99 per pack of 20.

Custom Tags are easy to specify too. You choose your own font and graphics from the online library and complete a detailed specification form for the layout and text you require. Examples are shown (customised wedding tags for example) and you can request a sample to be sent to you. Standard price starts at $50.00 for 100 tags, and $165.00 for 500, though you can upgrade to fancier designs.

Promotional Tags are available for corporate events, fundraisers or promotional giveaways. These can be customised with logos as required and prices are available on request.

A very specialised but attractive product, and the website makes choosing or putting together a custom design very simple.

---

www.kwagga.de/mab/wein/weinetab.htm
The Wine Label Gallery

Overall rating: ★ ★ ★			
Classification:	Enthusiasts	Readability:	★ ★
Updating:	Regularly	Content:	★ ★ ★
Navigation:	★ ★ ★	Speed:	★ ★ ★

G

Manfred Becker is a German wine and food enthusiast whose German language site covers his hobby generally. One of his big things is wine labels, and this part of the site has been translated into English too. The collection of labels here spans the globe, and each wine featured is accompanied by a high quality illustation of the label. Navigation is a little awkward, as the home page link takes you back to Becker's main page in German. The site uses an index frame down the left hand edge of the screen, and there is always a link to The Wine Label Gallery at the top of each regional index.

SPECIAL FEATURES

Labels are indexed by country and region, the index appearing in a frame down the left hand edge of the screen. When a region is selected, the list of available labels is displayed. Choose your label, click on it, and the image will appear in the right hand frame. One nice feature is a link that appears alongside some of the labels. It appears as a symbol of a building which, when clicked, will take you to the website for the winery. Herr Becker is also on the lookout for label swapping partners, and those labels he has on offer are marked with another little symbol.

OTHER FEATURES

Includes a couple of English language sections. At the bottom of the index frame you will find **Vintage Ratings** for most of the world's major wine regions. There is also a section of the site devoted to the country, food and tourism of East Frisia, Becker's home.

There's a friendly and heart-warming hyper-enthusiasm about this site. Like many collectors, Becker's obvious joy in his coveted collection of labels is apparent. There are lots of images gathered here, and it is an ideal stopping-off point for those that share his interest.

www.mitchell-beazley.co.uk/wine
Mitchell Beazley's World of Wine

Overall rating:	★★		
Classification:	Publisher	Readability:	★★★
Updating:	Rarely	Content:	★
Navigation:	★★★★	Speed:	★★★

(UK)

So near and yet so far. There's a sadly half-abandoned feel about this site from the world's biggest publisher of wine books. You can almost blow away the cobwebs on sections like Authors' Events which, well in to the year 2000, begins with '1999 events will follow shortly.' So why is the site here? Well, it has some very good reference material in the shape of an extensive set of extracts from Hugh Johnson's Story of Wine, as well as one or two other worthwhile features.

SPECIAL FEATURES

All About Wine is a sizeable chunk of Hugh Johnson's excellent book, The Story of Wine, complete with useful charts, illustrations and photographs. Chapters include: The Evolution of Modern Wine; Designing a Vineyard; Terroir; A Winemaker's Calendar; Wine and Time; Tasting and Talking About Wine and Looking After Wine. Each contains a lengthy extract from the book's text and key illustrations. In A Winemaker's Calendar for example, there is a very nicely done grid showing the work that goes on in vineyard and cellar throughout the winemaker's year. In Designing a Vineyard there are lovely drawings of the different training systems employed to suit vineyard conditions. This is a useful appetite whetter for the book, but for many people simply visiting or printing off these pages will be ample information.

Wine Books contains a list of several dozen titles complete with a brief synopsis and the opportunity to purchase. This is not a true ecommerce site however, as all you do is generate an order form to be faxed or posted.

Wine Tours also sounds more exciting than it actually is. It promises interactive tours of Provence and Tuscany, but the interactivity turns out to be nothing more than clicking on a rather crudely-rendered map in order to turn the virtual page to the next brief text extract.

OTHER FEATURES

There's a small list of **Wine Links**; **Connoisseurs**, an introduction to Mitchell Beazley's authors and a **Wine Forum** that is not terribly active.

Mitchell Beazley could surely do a lot more to encourage loyal visitors given their resources and the wonderful body of work contained in their titles. As it is, The Story of Wine makes the site well worth a visit if you don' t already own the book, but not much else does.

---

www.winemaster.com.au
Wine Master Board Game

Overall rating: ★ ★			
Classification:	Wine Game	Readability:	★ ★
Updating:	Rarely	Content:	★ ★
Navigation:	★ ★ ★ ★	Speed:	★ ★ ★ ★

AUS

Wine Master is a fun wine-based board game. It is part Trivial Pursuit, part blind tasting challenge and can be played by any number of people. The website is a few simple promotional pages and order form, but there is plenty of information and illustrations to give you a flavour for the product. The small, green navigation panel appears at the top of every screen making the site simple to use. The game costs $69.00 Australian and international shipping adds $15.00. This is not a full ecommerce site, so although the onscreen order form may be sent with credit card details these are not on a secure server. Alternatively, print it out and send by fax or post.

SPECIAL FEATURES

How to Play explains what the game is all about. The questions are multiple-choice and cover categories such as General Knowledge, Wine Terminology and Grape Varieties. The sensory component adds a special dimension to this game, where you and your guests can sample and analyse a specially selected wine. 'Palate of the Night' allows handicapping for those not so erudite on things vinous, whilst something called 'random cards' lends an element of chance. As the game is designed for a social setting the board is printed on cloth so it can be spread on the dinner table with wine glasses primed ready for action.

Play Now is a nice idea: a little teaser section taken from the quiz element of the game, with eight multiple choice wine questions that are scored instantly.

There isn't much to the website, but it does give you a feel for what the game is all about and the product might appeal. The little quiz adds a touch of interest for wine trivia buffs.

OTHER SITES OF INTEREST

Jancis Robinson's Wine Course
www.wellmedia.com/wine
Sales site for Jancis Robinson's superb video series, with some online content.

Vinoté
www.vinote.com
Vinoté is a wine storage and inventory system, designed to track and control wine in private cellars by use of numbered tags and a corresponding index book and software. (New Zealand, but ships to the UK at £19.95)

Vintage Cellars
www.vintagecellars.com
US company selling racking systems, but has very good How to Build a Cellar advice.

Glossary of Internet Terms

A

Accelerators Add-on programs, which speed up browsing.

Acceptable Use Policy These are the terms and conditions of using the internet. They are usually set by organisations, who wish to regulate an individual's use of the internet. For example, an employer might issue a ruling on the type of email which can be sent from an office.

Access Provider A company which provides access to the internet, usually via a dial-up account. Many companies such as AOL and Dircon charge for this service, although there are an increasing number of free services such as Freeserve, Lineone and Tesco.net. Also known as an Internet Service Provider.

Account A user's internet connection, with an Access/Internet Service Provider, which usually has to be paid for.

Acrobat Reader Small freely-available program, or web browser plug-in, which lets you view a Portable Document Format (PDF) file.

Across Lite Plug-in which allows you to complete crossword puzzles online.

Address Location name for email or internet site, which is the online equivalent of a postal address. It is usually composed of a unique series of words and punctuation, such as *my.name@myhouse.co.uk*. See also URL.

America Online (AOL) World's most heavily subscribed online service provider.

Animated GIF Low-grade animation technique used on websites.

ASCII Stands for American Standard Code for Information Interchange, It is a coding standard which all computers can recognise, and ensures that if a character is entered on one part of the internet, the same character will be seen elsewhere.

ASCII Art Art made of letters and other symbols. Because it is made up of simple text, it can be recognised by different computers.

ASDL Stands for Asynchronous Digital Subscriber Line, which is a high speed copper wire which will allow rapid transfer of information. Not widely in use at moment, though the government is pushing for its early introduction.

Attachment A file included with an email, which may be composed of text, graphics and sound. Attachments are encoded for transfer across the internet, and can be viewed in their original form by the recipient. An attachment is the equivalent of putting a photograph with a letter in the post.

B

Bookmark A function of the Netscape Netvigator browser which allows you to save a link to your favourite web pages, so that you can return straight there at a later date, without having to re-enter the address. Favourites in internet Explorer is the same thing.

BPS Abbreviation of Bits Per Second, which is a measure of the speed at which information is transferred or downloaded.

Browse Common term for looking around the web. See also Surfing.

Browser A generic term for the software that allows users to move and look around the Web. Netscape Navigator and Internet Explorer are the ones that most people are familiar with, and they account for 97 percent of web hits.

Bulletin Board Service A BBS is a computer with a telephone connection, which allows you direct contact to upload and download information and converse with other users, via the computer. It was the forerunner to the online services and virtual communities of today.

C

Cache A temporary storage space on the hard drive of your computer, which stores downloaded websites. When you return to a website, information is retrieved from the cache and displayed much more rapidly. However, this information may not be the most recent version for sites which are frequently updated and you will need to reload the Website address for these.

Chat Talking to other users on the web in real time, but with typed, instead of spoken words. Special software such as ICQ or MIRC is required before you can chat.

Chat Room An internet channel which allows several people to type in their messages, and talk to one another over the internet.

Clickstream The trail left as you 'click' your way around the web.

Content The material on a website that actually relates to the site, and is hopefully of interest or value. Things like adverts are not considered to be part of the content. The term is also used to refer to information on the internet that can be seen by users, as opposed to programming and other background information.

Cookie A cookie is a nugget of information sometimes sent by websites to your hard drive when you visit. They contain such details as what you looked at, what you ordered, and can add more information, so that the website can be customized to suit you.

Cybercafe Cafe where you can use a computer terminal to browse the net for a small fee.

Cyberspace When first coined by the sci-fi author William Gibson, it meant a shared hallucination which occured when people logged on to computer networks. Now, it refers to the virtual space you're in when on the internet.

D

Dial Up A temporary telephone connection to your ISP's computer and how you make contact with your ISP, each time you log onto the Internet.

Domain The part of an Internet address which identifies an individual computer, and can often be a business or person's name. For example, in the goodwebguide.com the domain name is theGoodWebGuide.

Download Transfer of information from an Internet server to your computer.

Dynamic HTML The most recent version of the HTML standard.

E

Ecash Electronic cash, used to make transactions on the internet.

Ecommerce The name for business which is carried out over the internet.

Email Mail which is delivered electronically over the

internet. They are usually comprised of text messages, but can contain illustrations, music and animations. Mail is sent to an email address, which is the internet equivalent of a postal address.

Encryption A process whereby information is scrambled to produce a 'coded message', so that it can't be read whilst in transit on the internet. The recipient must have decryption software in order to read the message.

Expire Term referring to newsgroup postings which are automatically deleted after a fixed period of time.

Ezine Publication on the web, which is updated regularly.

F

FAQ Stands for frequently asked questions and is a common section on websites where the most common enquiries and their answers are archived.

Frame A method which splits web pages into several windows.

FTP/File Transfer Protocol Standard method for transporting files across the internet.

G

GIF/Graphics Interchange Format A format in which graphics are compressed, and a popular method of putting images onto the internet, as they take little time to download.

Gopher The gopher was the precursor of the world wide web and consisted of archives accessed through a menu, usually organised by subject.

GUI/Graphical User Interface. This is the system which turns binary information into the words and images format you can see on your computer screen. For example, instead of seeing the computer language which denotes the presence of your toolbar, you actually see a toolbar.

H

Hackers A term used to refer to expert programmers who used their skills to break into computer systems, just for the fun of it. Nowadays the word is more commonly associated with computer criminals, or Crackers.

Header Basic indication of what's in an email: who it's from, when it was sent, and what it's about.

Hit When a file is downloaded from a website it is referred to as a 'hit'. Measuring the number of hits is a rough method of counting how many people visit a website. Except that it's not wholly accurate as one website can contain many files, so one visit by an individual may generate several hits.

Homepage Most usually associated with a personal site, produced by an individual, but can also refer to the first page on your browser, or the first page of a website.

Host Computer on which a website is stored. A host computer may store several websites, and usually has a fast powerful connection to the internet. Also known as a Server.

HTML/Hypertext Mark-Up Language The computer code used to construct web pages.

HTTP/Hypertext Transfer Protocol The protocol for moving HTML files across the web.

Hyperlink A word or graphic formatted so that when you click on it, you move from one area to another. See also hypertext.

Hypertext Text within a document which is formatted so it acts as a link from one page to another, or from one document to another.

I

Image Map A graphic which contains hyperlinks.

Interface What you actually see on the computer screen.

Internet One or more computers connected to one another is an internet (lower case i). The Internet is the biggest of all the internets. and consists of a worldwide collection of interconnected computer networks.

Internet Explorer One of the most popular pieces of browser software, produced by Microsoft.

Intranet A network of computers, which works in the same way as an internet, but for internal use, such as within a corporation.

ISDN/Integrated Services Digital Network Digital telephone line which facilitates very fast connections and can transfer larges amounts of data. It can carry more than one form of data at once.

ISP/Internet Service Provider See Access Provider.

J

Java Programming language which can be used to create interactive multimedia effects on webpages. The language is used to create programmes known as *applets* that add features such as animations, sound and even games to websites.

Javascript A scripting language which, like Java, can be used to add extra multimedia features. However, in contrast with Java it does not consist of separate programmes. Javascript is embedded into the HTML text and can interpreted by the browser, provided that the user has a javascript enabled browser.

JPEG Stands for 'Joint Photographic Experts Group' and is the name given to a type of format which compresses photos, so that they can be seen on the web.

K

Kill file A function which allows a user to block incoming information from unwanted sources. Normally used on email and newsreaders.

L

LAN/Local Area Network A type of internet, but limited to a single area, such as an office.

Login The account name or password needed to access a computer system.

Link Connection between web pages, or one web document and another, which are accessed via formatted text and graphic.

M

Mailing List A discussion group which is associated with a website. Participants send their emails to the site, and it is copied and sent by the server to other individuals on the mailing list.

Modem A device for converting digital data into analogue signals for transmission along standard phone lines. The usual way for home users to connect to the internet or log into their email accounts. May be internal (built into the computer) or external (a desk-top box connected to the computer).

MP3 A compressed music file format, which has almost no loss of quality although the compression rate may be very high.

N

Netscape Popular browser, now owned by AOL.

Newbie Term for someone new to the Internet. Used perjoratively of newcomers to bulletin boards or chat, who commit the sin of asking obvious questions or failing to observe the netiquette.

Newsgroup Discussion group amongst Internet users who share a mutual interest. There are thousands of newsgroups covering every possible subject.

O

Offline Not connected to the internet via a telephone line.

Online Connected to the internet via a telephone line.

Offline Browsing A function of the browser software, which allows the user to download pages and read them whilst offline.

Online Service Provider Similar to an access provider, but provides addtional features such as live chat.

P

PDF/Portable Document Format A file format created by Adobe for offline reading of brochures, reports and other documents with complex graphic design, which can be read by anyone with Acrobat Reader.

Plug-in Piece of software which adds more functions (such as playing music or video) to another, larger software program.

POP3/Post Office Protocol An email protocol that allows you to pick up your mail from any location on the web.

Portal A website which offers many services, such as search engines, email and chat rooms, and to which people are likely to return to often . ISPs such as Yahoo and Alta Vista provide portal sites which are the first thing you see when you log on, and in theory act as gateways to the rest of the web.

Post/Posting Information sent to a usenet group, bulletin board, message board or by email.

PPP/Point to Point Protocol The agreed way of sending data over dial-up connections, so that the user's computer, the modem and the Internet Server can all recognise it. It is the protocol which allows you to get online.

Protocol Convention detailing a set of actions that computers in a network must follow so that they can understand one another.

Q

Query Request for specific information from a database.

R

RAM /Random Access Memory Your computer's short term memory.

Realplayer G2 A plug-in program that allows you to view video in real-time and listen to sound and which is becoming increasingly important for web use.

Router A computer program which acts as an interface between two networks, and decides how to route information.

S

Searchable Database A database on a website which allows the user to search for information, usually be keyword.

Search Engine Programs which enable web users to search for pages and sites using keywords. They are usually to be found on portal sites and browser homepages. Infoseek, Alta Vista and Lycos are some of the popular search engines.

Secure Transactions Information transfers which are encrypted so that only the sender and recipient have access to the uncoded message, so that the details within remain private. The term is most commonly used to refer to credit card transactions, although other information can be sent in a secure form.

Server A powerful computer that has a permanent fast connection to the internet. Such computers are usually owned by companies and act as host computers for websites.

Sign-on To connect to the internet and start using one of its facilities.

Shareware Software that doesn't have to be paid for or test version of software that the user can access for free, as a trial before buying it.

Standard A style which the whole of the computer industry has agreed upon. Industry standards mean that hardware and software produced by the various different computer companies will work with one another.

Surfing Slang for looking around the Internet, without any particular aim, following links from site to site.

T

TLA/Three Letter Acronyms Netspeak for the abbreviations of net jargon, such as BPS (Bits Per Second) and ISP (Internet Service Provider).

U

Upload To send files from your computer to another one on the internet. When you send an email you are uploading a file.

URL/Uniform Resource Locator Jargon for an address on the internet, such as www.thegoodwebguide.co.uk.

Usenet A network of newsgroups, which form a worldwide system, on which anyone can post 'news'.

V

Virtual Community Name given to a congregation of regular mailing list/ newsgroup users.

VRML/Virtual Reality Modeling Language Method for creating 3D environments on the web.

W

Wallpaper Description of the sometimes hectic background patterns which appear behind the text on some websites.

Web Based Email/Webmail Email accounts such as Hotmail and Rocketmail, which are accessed via an Internet browser, rather than an email program such as Outlook Express. Webmail has to be typed whilst the user is online, but can accessed from anywhere on the Web.

Webmaster A person responsible for a web server. May also be known as System Administrator.

Web Page Document which forms one part of a website (though some sites are a single page), usually formatted in HTML.

Web Ring Loose association of websites which are usually dedicated to the same subject and often contain links to one another.

Website A collection of related web pages which often belong to an individual or organisation and are about the same subject.

World Wide Web The part of the Internet which is easy to get around and see. The term is often mistakely interchanged with Internet, though the two are not the same. If the Internet is a shopping mall, with shops, depots, and delivery bays, then the web is the actual shops which the customers see and use.

A

Albert Bichot 67
Alsace (web site) 91
Amazon 72
Antinori 105
Antique Wine Company, the 66-67
Anvar Tasting Club, the 35
Arblaster & Clarke Wine Tours 133-134
Argentinean Wine Page, the 93
Art of Wine, the 140-141
Ata Rangi 112
Australian Society of Wine Education 132
Australian Wine Industry Journal, the 92
Australian Wine Online 92

B

Bailey, Richard 36
Bailey, Toby 36
Bava 106
Becker, Dirk 82
Bedini, Mark 52
Berlinger Vineyards 110
Berry Brothers and Rudd 55
Beverage Tasting Institute 121
Bibendum 56
Bipin's Wine Notes 19
Boehmer, Alan
Bolla 106
Bonterra Vineyards 110
books 11, 24, 29, 54, 121, 136
Bordeaux;
  region 20
  wine 58, 59, 67, 101, 104
  web site 91
Bordeaux Direct 57
Boschendal Wines South Africa 112
bottle sizes 37, 41

Bottoms Up 60-61
Bouchard Père et Fils 104
British Wines 88
Broadbent, Michael 120
Brown, Bradford 15
Brown Brothers Wines 100
Bulgarian Wine Guild 93
Burgundy;
  region 18, 102
  wine 67, 104
Buscke, Maree 83

C

California Wine 84-85
Cambridge Wine 72
Cannavan, Tom 10, 11
Casa Lapostolle 111
Castello Banfi 106
Cave Cru Classé 72
Cephas Picture Library 135
Chablis;
  region 18
Champagne;
  region (website) 91
  wine 60, 73, 103, 105
Champagne Lanson 105
Champagne Perrier-Jouët 105
Champagne Veuve Clicquot 105
Chandos Deli 72
Chanson Père et Fils 104
Chapoutier 105
Charles Heidsieck 28
Charles Joguet 105
Château Cos d'Estournel 104
Château de la Tuilerie 105
Château des Charmes 110
Château d'Yquem 104

Château Figeac 104
Château Hajji Firuz 45
Château Haut-Brion 100-101
Château Lafite Rothschild 104
Château Latour 104
Château Lynch-Bages 104
Château Margaux 19, 104
Château Musar 34, 107
Château Pichon-Longueville 104
ChateauOnline 59
Cheval Blanc 18
China Wine 94
Christoph, Justin 37
Christoph's Quarterly 37
claret 20, 36
Classic Wines (website) 72
Cline Cellars 110
Cloudy Bay 112
Coates, Clive 72, 120, 122
Columbia Crest 110
Coppola, Francis Ford 19
cork 47
Corrigan, Andrew 93m
Côte Chalonnaise 18
Croatian Wine Page 94
Croft Port 112
Cuchet, Bud 52

D

Daily Wine Review 48
De Bortoli Wines 100
Decanter (magazine) 116, 128, 135
Deluc, Jean Michel 59
Denbies Wine Estate 113
Desai, Bipin 19
Domaine Dujac 104
Domaine Jean-Marc Brocard 104

Domaine Laroche 104
Domaine Rossignol-Trapet 104
Dom Perignon 29
Dopff 'Au Moulin' 105
Dr Loosen 112
Duval, John 99

E

English wines 88
Enjoyment 60
Epernay 103
ErrazurizChile 111

F

Far Niente 110
Foodmad 126
Fustino 113
Ferrari-Carano Vineyards 110
Fetzer Vineyards 110
First Quench 60
Flichman Argentina 111
Fonseca Guimaraens 112

G

Gabryelski, Keith 22
Gang of Pour 48
Garr, Robin 16, 17
Georges Duboeuf 104
German Wine Page, the 86-87
Gidleigh Park 48
Gilbeys 42
glassware 137
González Byass 113
Goode, Jamie 23
grape varieties 26
Greek Wine (website)

H

Halliday, James 83, 117
Harvey-Jones, Richard 71
Hatch-Mansfield 108
Hawkins, Anthony J. 32
Henry of Pelham Family Estate Winery 110
Hochar, Gaston 107
Hochar, Serge 107
Hogue Cellars 110
Hugel et Fils 105

I

Inglis, Ken 43
Inniskillin Wines 110
Irish Wine Page, the 41
Italian D. O. C. Wines 87

J

Jackson Estate 112
James Nicholson 72
Jancis Robinson's Wine Course 145
John Gilman's Wine Vault 48
John Roberts Wine Books 136
Johnson, Arthur P. 29
Jones, Andrew 28
Joseph Drouhin 102

K

Kékfrankos 34
Kincaid, Les 46
Klein Constantia Estate South Africa 112

L

La Baume 105
Lafite 20
Laithwaite, Tony 57
Lapsley, George M. 40
Lapsley, James T. 40
La Rioja Alta 113
Lay and Wheeler 73
Laytons 73
L'Ecole No 41 110
Lehmusvuori, Hannu 49
Lenz Moser
Les Kincaid's Lifestyles 46
Lingenfelder Estate 112
Loire Valley (website) 91
Louis Latour 104

M

Mâconnais, the 18
madaboutwine 52
magazines 115
Maison de Pierre 67
Majestic Wine Warehouses 73
Mark Squires E-zine on Wine 20
Marsovin Wines 94
Martínez Bujanda 113
May, Peter 34
McGovern, Patrick 45
Mentzelopoulos, Corinne 19
Merryvale Vineyards 110
Mildara Blass Wines 100
Mitchell Beazley's Worldof Wine 143-144
Moët & Chandon 103
Montrachet 18
Mouton Rothschild 20, 53
Muir, Gordon 44
Murray, Alex 56

N

Niebaum-Coppola 110
Noble, Professor Anne 40
Noel Young Wines 72

Norrie, Dr Philip 47
Norton Argentina 111

O

On Wine 129
Origins and Ancient history of Wine 45
Oz Clarke 129

P

Park Lane Champagne 73
Paramount Picture 66
Parker, Robert 11, 128-129
Paul Jaboulet Aîné 105
Payne and Rayner Wines 68-69
Penfolds 98-99
Peter Wylie Fine Wines 73
Petrini, Carlo 25
Philadelphia Sun, the 37
Pichon Lalande 20
Pinotage Club 48
port 21-22
Portuguese Wine (website) 94
Port Wine (website) 22
Preamble Club, the 41
Provence (website) 91

Q

Quarterly Review of Wines, the 120
Quinta de la Rosa 112

R

Raeburn Fine Wines 73
Ravenswood 110
Red and White Wine Company 70-71
red wines 33
Reichsgraff von Kesselstatt 112
R. F. Buller & Son 67-68

Rhône Valley (website) 91
Rhurberg, Peter 86
Richardson, Oliver 88
Ridge Vineyards 110
Riedel 137
Rioja;
  region 82
  wine 82, 113
Rioja Wine Shop, the 82
Ritz-Carlton Hotel, the 120
Robert Mondavi 108
Robinson, Jancis 38 , 120, 145
Rocca delle Macie 106
Rogov, Daniel 26
Romanian Wines 94
Rosemount Estates 100
Ruffino 106

S

Sandeman 112
Santa Carolina (wine) 68
Schloss Gobelsburg 111
Schubert, Max 99
Seckford Wines 71-72
Shaya, Yak 18
Slow Food Guide to Wine 25
Smart Wine 129
South African Wine Directory 80-81
Southern Wine Brands 68
Southwest France (website) 91
Spanish Wine Page, the 82
Squires, Mark 20, 21
Stratermeyer, Art 26
Stratermeyer, Betsy 26
Strat's Place 26
Sunday Times Wine Club, the 57, 73, 134
Super Gigantic Winegrape Glossary, the 32

Swiss Wine Page, the 95

T

Table Wine (website) 48
Tan, Simon 33
Tastings.com 121
Taylor's Port 18
Terrabianca 106
TBM's Wine Links 27
Three Choirs 113
Toby Bailey's Tasting Notes 36
Tom Cannavan's Wine Pages 10
Torres 113

U

ullage 37, 63
University of Bath, the 16
University of California Davis 39
University of Glasgow, the 10, 108
Unusual Wines 34

V

Valvona and Crolla 73
Victoria Wine 60
Vieux Château Certan 104
Vine, the 122
Vine2Wine 14-15
Vineyards and Wine-making in England and Wales 88-89
Vinifera Wine Pages 43
Vinopolis Wine Exhibition 134
Vinoté 145
Vinprom-Svishtov 111
Viña Santa Rita Chile 111
Vintage Cellars 145
Virtual Corkscrew Museum, the 138-139
vitis labruscana 32

vitis vinifera 32
volatile acidity 40

W

Waterhouse, Dr. Andrew 40
WeekendWines.com 125-126
Weingut Carl Von Schubert 112
Weingut Gunderloch Nackenheim 112
Weingut Kurt Darting 112
Welsh wines 88
West Coast Wine 48
Whitcombe, Tim 48
White, Paul 31
white wines 33
Willamette Valley Vineyards 110
Wine Advocate, the 128-129
Wine and Spirit Association 48
Wine and Spirit Education Trust (WSET), the 38
Wine Anorak, the 23
wine appreciation 13-49
wine auctions 62-65
Winebid 62-63
Wine Base 132-133
Wine Brats 129
Wine Club Ansvar 35
Wine.com 48
Wine Enthusiast 124-125
Wine FAQ, the 15-16
Wine Glass Name Tags 141
wine grapes 32
Wine Label Gallery, the 143-144
wine labels 26, 34, 86, 143-144
Wine Lovers' page, the 16-17
Winemaker 127-128
Winemaking Home Page 49
Wine Master Board Game 144-145
wine merchants 23, 51-73

Wine News, the 116-117
Wine of the Week 49
Wine of the Week (New Zealand) 83, 84
Wine of Tokaji 94
Wine On the Web 28
Wineorama 63-64
Wine-Owners.com 64-65
Wine People 29
Wine Place, the 33
Wine Press Northwest 129
Wine Pros 117-118
Wineraks 73
wine regions;
  Argentina 93, 110
  Austria 93, 111
  Australia 24, 92-93, 98-100, 117
  Belgium 89
  Bulgaria 93, 111
  Canada 93, 110
  Chile 94, 110
  China 94
  Croatia 94
  Eire 89
  France 18, 24, 90-91
  Germany 86-87, 112
  Greece 94, 112
  Holland 89
  Hungary 94
  Italy 42, 87
  Lebanon 34, 107
  Malta 93
  New Zealand 83-84, 112
  Portugal 22, 95, 112
  Romania 94
  Scandinavia 89
  Singapore 33
  Spain 82-83, 113
  South Africa 80-81, 112-113
  Switzerland 95
  United Kingdom 88-89, 112
  USA 21, 24, 84-85, 110
  Zimbabwe 95
wineries 25, 97-113
Winery Skouras 112
Wines and Food from France 90-91
Winesearcher 54
Wine Sense 31
Wines from Austria (website) 93
Wines of Canada 93
Wines of Chile 93
Wines of the Internet 49
Wine Spectator 118-119
Wine State 129
wine tastings 27, 41;
  how to hold 26, 33
Wine Technologies — Robert Parker's Wine Software 139-140
Wine Today 123
Wine X 129
Wynns Coonwarra Estate 100

X

Xinomavro 34

Y

Yak Shaya's Wine Page 18
Yapp Brothers 73
Yquem 18

Z

Zimbabwean Wine Page, the 95

How to use your CD

Now we've whetted your appetite for the sites reviewed in this book, we can help you to visit them quickly and easily. By registering on thegoodwebguide site, you will be able to use the hotlinks to all the sites listed, so you just click and go. You can also read the latest versions of reviews and see what we think of new sites that have been launched since the book went to press. If you wish, you can even have the updates emailed to you.

INSTALLATION INSTRUCTIONS FOR PC USERS
Insert the CD enclosed with this book into your CD drive of your PC. A welcome screen will appear with two buttons:

The goodwebguide button To register your purchase of a Good Web Guide book and to receive free updates of the reviews in the book and reviews of the latest sites, click on this button. When you've registered you can click straight through to any of the sites listed. You must have an internet connection to do this. If you are not already signed up with an internet service, you will need to install the LineOne software first.

If you click on the goodwebguide button you will be taken to a registration page where you will be asked to confirm which title in the series you have bought and to register your details. You then have free access to the updates of the website reviews in this book and to new reviews. You will also have access to the rest of the goodwebguide website.

LineOne button If you would like access to the internet you can click on this button to install LineOne's free ISP (internet service provider) software. You will need a modem to have internet access. If you already have an internet connection (ISP) you can still install LineOne as an alternative provider.

A To join LineOne just click on the LineOne button. When the first screen appears you have a choice: If you are a new user and wish to load Internet Explorer 5 as your browser, select 'Join Now'. On the next screen, select 'Go!' and you will be taken to the Microsoft installation process.

B To join immediately, without installing a browser, click 'Join Now' and then choose 'custom' to go straight to registration.

From the 'Welcome to LineOne' screen, click 'Go' and follow the on-screen instructions.

MAC USERS
This CD is not suitable for Apple Macintosh computers. For Free LineOne Mac Software call free on 0800 111 210.

RETURNING TO THE GOOD WEB GUIDE
Once you've connected to the internet, you can either type www.thegoodwebguide.co.uk into your browser to go directly to our website, or re-insert your CD and click on the goodwebguide button.

SUPPORT
If you have any problems call the LineOne support number.
CALL 0906 30 20 100
(calls may be monitored or recorded for training purposes) 24 hours, 365 days a year. Calls charged at 50p/minute or email support@lineone.net for free support.

Other great titles in thegoodwebguide series:

Money	Gardening	Food	Parents
ISBN 1-903282-02-0	ISBN 1-903282-00-4	ISBN 1-903282-01-2	ISBN 1-903282-03-9

Genealogy	Travel	Wine	Health
ISBN 1-903282-06-3	ISBN 1-903282-05-5	ISBN 1-903282-04-7	ISBN 1-903282-08-X